WAR WITH HANNIBAL

WAR WITH HANNIBAL

Authentic Latin Prose for the Beginning Student

Brian Beyer

Yale University Press
New Haven & London

Publisher: Mary Jane Peluso
Editorial Assistant: Elise Panza
Project Editor: Timothy Shea
Production Editor: Ann-Marie Imbornoni
Production Controller: Karen Stickler
Designer: Nancy Ovedovitz
Maps by Bill Nelson.
Set by Keystone Typesetting.
Printed in the United States of America.

Library of Congress Cataloging-in-Publication Data

Eutropius, 4th cent.
[Breviarium ab urbe condita. Liber 3]
War with Hannibal : authentic Latin prose for the beginning student / [annotated by] Brian Beyer.
p. cm.
Unabridged Latin text of Book III of Eutropius's Breviarium ab urbe condita; notes and commentary in English.
Includes bibliographical references and index.
ISBN 978-0-300-13918-1 (pbk. : alk. paper)
1. Punic War, 2nd, 218–201 B.C. 2. Hannibal, 247–182 B.C. 3. Rome—History—Republic, 265–30 B.C. 4. Carthage (Extinct city)—History. 5. Latin language—Readers. I. Beyer, Brian, 1966– II. Title.
PA6384.A2 2009
871′.01—dc22   2008013291

A catalogue record for this book is available from the British Library.

10 9 8 7 6 5 4 3 2 1

To the memory of Michael R. Paley, whose help with this project was of inestimable value and whose friendship will be sorely missed

[T]he war which I am going to describe was the most memorable of all wars ever waged—the war, that is, which, under the leadership of Hannibal, the Carthaginians waged with the Roman People. For neither have states or nations met in arms possessed of ampler resources, nor was their own might and power ever so great. Nor yet were they strangers to one another's modes of fighting, which the First Punic War had made them understand. And so variable were the fortunes of the war and so uncertain was its outcome that those who ultimately conquered had been nearer ruin.

—Livy, *Ab urbe condita* 21.1, translated by B. O. Foster

The importance of the Second Punic War can hardly be exaggerated. It was a turning point in the history of the whole ancient world. Its effect on Rome and Italy, on the constitution, on economic life, on religion and thought was profound. After it no power arose that could endanger the existence of Rome. The Hellenistic monarchs of the east still flourished, but at Rome's touch they fell like a house of cards. She was mistress of the fortunes of the civilized world and gradually introduced into that world a unity, unknown since the days of Alexander, which lasted some five hundred years. Further, the dramatic nature of the struggle has captivated the imagination of mankind. . . . Never did the spirit of the Roman people shine forth brighter than in the dark hours of the Second Punic War.

—H. H. Scullard, *A History of the Roman World 753–146 BC*

CONTENTS

FOREWORD

After we've traversed that desolate country of introductory grammar with our students, we're ready for some relief. We want to show them that Latin is more than just an endless puzzle of syntactical problems, that there's more in our own minds than participles and fourscore uses of the subjunctive mood, and that their diligent study of a difficult language has finally led them to something worth talking about. But something goes wrong. At the threshold of real authors and real Latin, they find the door bolted even still, and our classes grind back down to a laborious and uninspiring slog through more and more grammar. We all know this is true. We share our stories over drinks at conferences.

We're somewhat forced into this because we're aware that the clock is always ticking. Most universities have a threadbare language requirement, after which the mass exodus begins. That means if we want to leave them with a favorable impression of Latin and classics—and of classicists, for that matter—we have to get to real issues and real authors sooner than we should. We each find our own way and hope for the best.

Beyer's edition of Eutropius is a most welcome addition to the spread of texts that address this problem. Eutropius writes in good, standard classical Latin, so we don't have to undo what we taught our students. His style is lucid and simple, without being insultingly juvenile. It challenges the emerging Latin students without annihilating their confidence, as Cicero does more often than not. Beyer supplements the readings with generous notes, which deftly point out the way without eliminating the little bit of pain that's necessary to leave students a sense of accomplishment when they've worked things out.

And Eutropius is not Cicero or Ovid or Caesar or Nepos or any of the other usual suspects whose works populate the third-semester syllabus. I have nothing against any of them, but on occasion I find even the best of students understandably uninspired by the endless tangle of ambitions that drove Roman politics or by the doings of yet another nymph or bear or randy god. The conversation flags.

The Second Punic War, by contrast, needs no introduction. Since Livy is impossible at this level, Eutropius is the perfect understudy, and Beyer's is an excellent edition. I am very glad to see it made available by Yale University Press, and I hope it finds its way into the curriculum of many Latin programs across the country.

Dale Grote
University of North Carolina, Charlotte

Preface

Why Eutropius?

There is hardly a more formidable task facing the beginning Latin student than the transition from the simplified Latin of a first-year textbook to the complex, periodic prose of the second-year curriculum. It is difficult to overstate how discouraging it can be to a student who has spent a year or more learning the basics of Latin to meet with an incomprehensible wall on his or her first attempt at reading a "real author." Anyone who has taught first- or second-year Latin knows there is a long-standing need for a suitable "bridge text" that will introduce students to reading extended prose and that will give them the skills and confidence necessary to go on to Caesar, Cicero, or a similar author.

This edition of Book III of Eutropius's *Breviarium ab urbe condita*, then, is not meant to replace any work currently read in schools or colleges. It is meant rather to be a student's first encounter with extended, unaltered Latin prose—a bridge between a textbook and those authors normally read during the second year. The *Breviarium* has, in fact, a long and distinguished career as such a "bridge text" (see Introduction, below). Indeed, it is difficult to imagine a text better suited to the linguistic needs of the beginning Latin student: the vocabulary consists almost exclusively of the most common Latin words, the prose is carefully constructed with a good deal of variation in syntax, the sentences are not overly lengthy or complex, and the narrative is simple and direct.

Book III of the *Breviarium* also covers the period of Roman history that students often find most interesting—the Second Punic War. In this edition, Eutropius's narrative is presented without any adaptations or omissions (with the exception of the first sentence, where an unrelated discussion of a war with the Istrians is deleted). The Latin text is supplemented by passages in English from other ancient authors, adding color and detail to the story. Historical notes—set off in boxes, for easy reference—are provided in the Commentary.

At the college level, it typically takes three to four weeks to read this text in its entirety (at the high-school level, of course, it will take longer). Thus it is ideally suited to be the "payoff" immediately after finishing an elementary textbook, or an opportunity for review and reinforcement at the beginning of year two. It may also be used as supplementary readings toward the end of a basal program—say, after chapter 28 in Wheelock or chapter 42 in *Ecce Romani*—with the material spread out over a longer period of time.

Format of This Edition

Since this text is meant to be a student's first encounter with continuous Latin prose, the amount of translation help given is quite liberal and comes in a number of forms. The most basic glosses—the ones most readers will need to "get" the Latin—appear at the bottom of the text pages, where they are easily accessible. More in-depth translation help, formal analyses of the grammar and syntax, and historical notes are placed in the Commentary section. This allows for an ample running commentary while leaving the simple glosses unencumbered.

The Commentary need not be read in its entirety, but may be referred to on an as-needed basis. As such, basic translation help and identification of perfect participles, subjunctives, and the like, are repeated over the course of the notes. More-lengthy discussions of grammar and syntax (e.g., regarding purpose and jussive noun clauses) take place only at their first occurrence in the text. Readers who would like to refer to these sections may easily do so by means of the Index of Selected Grammatical Constructions.

All grammatical principles in the Commentary are cross-referenced to the commonly used U.S. textbooks: *Wheelock's Latin*, 6th Edition, Revised

(New York: Harper Collins, 2005), *Latin: An Intensive Course* (Berkeley: University of California Press, 1977), *Ecce Romani II*, 3rd Edition (Upper Saddle River, N.J.: Prentice Hall, 2000), *Latin for Americans*, Level 2 (New York: Glencoe/McGraw-Hill, 2004), *Jenney's Second Year Latin* (Upper Saddle River, N.J.: Prentice Hall, 1990), as well as to the standard reference grammar, Allen and Greenough's *New Latin Grammar*. The latter is available online from the Perseus Digital Library at www.perseus.tufts.edu.

A section with only the bare Latin text has been included for use in the classroom. Not having the notes under the student's eye in the classroom ensures that the glosses are not used as a crutch and that grammatical concepts have been thoroughly learned. The inclusion of the bare text as a separate section allows the bottom-of-the-page glosses to be preserved in the Text and Notes section, which is more "user-friendly" for the student's initial contact with the text.

The Appendixes include a basic timeline of the Second Punic War, maps and battle plans, and a list of all Roman magistracies mentioned in this text, and the Bibliography gives a list of texts, commentaries, and translations. An Index of Selected Grammatical Constructions is included so that teachers may locate illustrative examples of particular constructions.

Vocabulary

The Vocabulary section has been compiled specifically for Book III of Eutropius's *Breviarium*. The entries have been adapted in part from Lewis and Short's *Latin Dictionary* (New York: Harper and Brothers, 1897), with changes made where necessary in accordance with Segoloni and Corsini's *Eutropii Lexicon* (Perugia: Studium generale civitatis Perusii, 1982).

The Vocabulary also contains a number of features helpful to the beginning student: all forms where the dictionary entry might not be immediately recognized (e.g., irregular perfects, perfect participles, etc.) are given individual entries pointing to the relevant lexical form; the elements of all compound words are shown in brackets; basic biographical information is included for all historical persons; entries are given for all forms of personal names that appear in the text (e.g., *praenomen* abbreviations);

references to specific passages in Book III of the *Breviarium* are given
where it seemed necessary to clarify the usage of a word. The inclusion of
all inflected forms of a word after the dictionary entry—an innovative fea-
ture in a Latin commentary—allows the student to confirm that he or she
has found the correct entry for a given word.

Latin Text

The established texts of the major critical editions (see Bibliography) differ
in only a few places in all of Book III of the *Breviarium*. The overarching
principle used for establishing the Latin text of this edition was that of
following the reading easiest for the beginning student. Because of the
nature of the work, discussions of manuscript variants have been kept to
the barest of minimums. Macrons have been added to the entire text in
accordance with the vowel quantities used in the *Oxford Latin Dictionary*
(New York: Oxford University Press, 1982).

ACKNOWLEDGMENTS

I wish to thank first and foremost Professor T. Corey Brennan of Rutgers University, without whose help and encouragement this project would still be in the "wouldn't it be great if . . ." stage, and Professor Dale Grote of University of North Carolina, Charlotte, for generously agreeing to write a foreword. I would also like to express my sincere gratitude to Jeremy Thompson, Anthony Stromoski, and especially Ryan Fowler for reading the entire manuscript and for their expert advice at all stages of this project. I also owe a deep debt of gratitude to Professor Leah Kronenberg for "field testing" the work in multiple sections of Latin 102 at Rutgers University and to the many students at Rutgers University, Princeton High School, and Montgomery High School who have provided invaluable feedback.

Special thanks are owed to the staff at Yale University Press, in particular Mary Jane Peluso, a publisher of exceeding insight and flexibility. The meticulous work of her editorial assistant, Elise Panza, has been very much appreciated, as has been the careful and expert hand of the production editor, Ann-Marie Imbornoni. Thanks are also owed to David Bright of Emory University and Randall Ganiban of Middlebury College who read the initial manuscript for the press.

Not least of all, I would like to thank Michael Greenberg for helping prepare the preliminary version of the manuscript and Barbara Grau for all of her friendly encouragement and practical advice. Above all else, though, I have to thank *eum qui dat lasso virtutem* for giving me the strength to get up at predawn hours every day to work on this project, and my loving wife, Ruth, for helping me to do so.

INTRODUCTION

This edition of Book III of Eutropius's *Breviarium ab urbe condita* presents authentic, unabridged Latin prose for the beginning student. The text's subject matter covers one of the most interesting and important periods in Roman history: the second of three wars Rome fought with Carthage. As background to the reading, summary descriptions of Rome's prior conquest of Italy and each of the three Punic Wars are below (*Punic* is from the Latin word for *Phoenician*, since the Carthaginians were descendants of Phoenician settlers). For detailed notes on the Second Punic War, see the Commentary.

Conquest of Italy

During the two centuries prior to its conflicts with Carthage, Rome had come to dominate nearly the entire Italian peninsula through a combination of conquest and diplomacy. It had come to terms with or defeated its principal neighbors in Etruria, Latium, Umbria, and Samnium and had established a complex and long-lasting network of alliances (the Greek cities of southern Italy were the last to succumb to Roman authority, which was to have significance in Rome's later struggles with Carthage). The strength of these alliances—and their capacity to supply the Romans with a seemingly endless supply of troops—was to be a critical factor in Rome's emergence as a world power. See Appendix B, Principal areas: Italy and Mediterranean environs.

First Punic War, 264–241 BCE

Carthage was a Phoenician colony on the northernmost coast of Africa that had established a trading empire in the western Mediterranean. Rome and Carthage had concluded treaty relations at various times between the sixth and fourth centuries, and Carthage had even aided Rome in the Pyrrhic War of 280–275 BCE. However, the positions of Rome and Carthage as the most important powers in the West made it inevitable that the two sides would become rivals. The First Punic War was fought between 264 and 241 BCE in an attempt to drive the Carthaginians from Sicily. The war was fought primarily at sea (the Romans were forced to build their first significant fleet of warships) with heavy casualties on both sides. The Romans slowly won the upper hand, however, and peace was concluded, with the Carthaginians agreeing to leave Sicily and to pay indemnity to Rome. A few years later, Rome succeeded in forcing the Carthaginians out of Sardinia and Corsica. The conclusion of the First Punic War thus marked the beginning of Roman administration of overseas provinces.

Second Punic War, 218–201 BCE

Twenty years of uneasy peace was broken in 219 BCE, when the Carthaginian general Hannibal besieged Saguntum, a Roman ally in Spain. Without waiting for a Roman declaration of war, he took the Romans by surprise by marching over the Alps into Italy with troops and war elephants. After initial Carthaginian victories, Q. Fabius Maximus Cunctator adopted a policy of harassing Hannibal's army and avoiding a general engagement. The abandonment of this stratagem resulted in devastating Roman losses at the Battle of Cannae in 216. From then on, the Romans pursued a policy of attrition in Italy, while aggressively prosecuting the war in Spain and Sicily and ensuring that Hannibal did not receive critical reinforcements. When the Romans invaded Africa in 203 under the command of P. Cornelius Scipio, the Carthaginians were forced to recall Hannibal from Italy. The Carthaginians under the command of Hannibal were defeated at the Battle of Zama in 202, and peace was concluded the following year. As with the conclusion of the First Punic War, Rome was now in possession of new overseas provinces, marking another step forward in its eventual conquest of the Mediterranean basin.

Third Punic War, 149–146 BCE

Carthage, however, made a remarkably quick economic recovery, and the animosity felt toward them by the Romans continued (perhaps most famously illustrated by the fact that the powerful Roman senator Marcus Porcius Cato ended every speech with *Carthago delenda est* [Carthage must be destroyed]). When Carthage attacked the Roman ally Masinissa in 150 BCE, Rome declared war the following year and sent an army to Africa. After a quick surrender, the Carthaginians refused the Roman demand to vacate their city. Carthage then endured a Roman siege until 146 BCE, when Scipio Aemilianus stormed and sacked the city. The city was destroyed, and its territory became the Roman province of Africa.

History of the *Breviarium ab urbe condita*

Eutropius's *Breviarium ab urbe condita*—from which the account of the Second Punic War in this text is taken—was written in the latter half of the fourth century CE, during the reign of the emperors Valens and Valentinian. The work, which consists of ten books, begins with the foundation of Rome in 753 BCE and ends with the death of the emperor Jovian in 364 CE. It was written for an aristocracy whose first language was often not Latin, and who needed a succinct and readable history of Rome. It immediately became popular both in the West and, in translation, in the Byzantine world. Its popularity in both the Middle Ages and the Renaissance is attested to by the survival of over eighty manuscripts, eleven from before the fifteenth century. The *Breviarium* even makes it onto Petrarch's short list of favorite books (*Libri mei peculiares*) from 1333.

In the modern era, the *Breviarium* became a staple of the school curriculum in both the United States and Britain, and was very often the first Latin text a student read. Many nineteenth-century educators regarded Caesar's

Commentarii de bello Gallico as too difficult for use as a first Latin text, and saw the *Breviarium* as an ideal "bridge text." The Report of the Committee of Twelve of the American Philological Association in 1899, for instance, suggests the use of Eutropius for reading just before Caesar. Similarly, Arrowsmith and Whicher's popular nineteenth-century reader includes an entire three books of Eutropius before moving on to Caesar.

The *Breviarium* enjoyed a publication history from the eighteenth through the early twentieth century comparable to or greater than almost any other Latin text read in schools. In 1902, for example, there were no fewer than fourteen different editions of the *Breviarium* in print in the United States and Britain. By contrast, the same year there was a combined total of only ten editions of all works by Nepos in print. Furthermore, a number of editions of Eutropius enjoyed continuous reprints throughout the first half of the twentieth century. It was not until the late 1950s (a time when there was a new emphasis on introducing increasingly adult-age Latin students to Cicero and similar writers as soon as possible) that the last school edition of the *Breviarium* finally went out of print.

Life of Eutropius

Little is known about the life of Eutropius. Apparently, he was from a wealthy but not senatorial family and was given a good education. He began a career as an imperial clerk under the emperor Constantine. We learn from a comment in the *Breviarium* itself that he served under the emperor Julian in his expedition against the Persians in 363 CE. Under the emperor Valens (to whom the *Breviarium* is dedicated), he was promoted to the senior imperial Secretariat (*magister memoriae*). His survey of Roman history is his only work that has been preserved.

Eutropius's
Breviarium
ab urbe condita,
Liber tertius

Hannibal at nine years of age swearing enmity to the Romans. Print Collection, Miriam and Ira D. Wallach Division of Art, Prints and Photographs, The New York Public Library, Astor, Lenox, and Tilden Foundations.

Text and Notes

Second Punic War commences; Hannibal lays siege to Saguntum

VII⌈M. Minuciō Rūfō P. Cornēliō consulibus⌋bellum Pūnicum secundum
Rōmānīs inlātum est per Hannibalem, Carthāginiēnsium ducem, quī Saguntum, Hispāniae cīvitātem Rōmānīs amīcam, obpugnāre adgressus est,
annum agēns vīcēsimum aetātis⌈cōpiīs congregātīs CL mīlium⌋Huic Rōmānī per lēgātōs dēnuntiāvērunt, ut bellō abstinēret. Is lēgātōs admittere   5
nōluit. Rōmānī etiam Carthāginem mīsērunt, ut mandārētur Hannibalī,

1. **M. Minuciō Rūfō P. Cornēliō consulibus** – *with Marcus Minucius Rufus
   [and] Publius Cornelius [Scipio Asina] being consuls = in the consulships of
   Marcus Minucius and Publius Cornelius.* Supply *et* between the two names.
   The year is 221 BCE.
2. **per Hannibalem** – *by Hannibal.*
3. **Rōmānīs amīcam** – *friendly to the Romans,* i.e., a Roman ally.
   obpugnāre adgressus est – *began to besiege.*
4. **annum agēns vīcēsimum aetātis** – *acting [in] the twentieth year of his age =
   at the age of nineteen.*
   cōpiīs congregātīs CL mīlium – *with a hundred and fifty thousand troops
   having been gathered together = after he had gathered together a hundred and
   fifty thousand troops.*
   Huic . . . dēnuntiāvērunt, ut bellō abstinēret – *brought orders to him that
   he should abstain from war = ordered him to abstain from war.*
6. **Rōmānī etiam Carthāginem mīsērunt** – supply *demands.*
   ut mandārētur Hannibalī, nē bellum . . . gereret – *that it might be
   commanded to Hannibal that he should not wage war = that Hannibal might
   be commanded not to wage war.*

nē bellum contrā sociōs populī Rōmānī gereret. Dūra responsa ā Carthāginiēnsibus data sunt. Saguntīnī intereā fame victī sunt, captīque ab Hannibale ultimīs poenīs adficiuntur.

POLYBIUS ON THE ROMAN AMBASSADORS AT CARTHAGE

The Roman ambassadors said nothing in response to the demands
of the Carthaginians. Instead, their senior member showed the
folds of his toga to the Carthaginian assembly and said that it held
for them both war and peace—he would let fall and leave with them
whichever of the two they requested. The Carthaginian suffect told
him to let fall whichever of the two seemed best to the Romans.
When the Roman ambassador said that war would fall, the majority
of the Carthaginian assembly cried out together that they accepted
it. The ambassadors and the assembly parted on these terms.

Histories 3.33, translated by B. Beyer

War declared against Carthage; Hannibal crosses the Alps

10   VIII. Tum P. Cornēlius Scīpiō cum exercitū in Hispāniam profectus est, Ti.
Semprōnius in Siciliam; bellum Carthāginiēnsibus indictum est. Hannibal, relictō in Hispāniā frātre Hasdrubale, Pȳrēnaeum transiit. Alpēs, adhūc eā parte inviās, sibi patefēcit. Trāditur ad Ītaliam LXXX mīlia peditum, X mīlia equitum, septem et XXX elephantōs addūxisse. Intereā multī
15   Ligurēs et Gallī Hannibalī sē coniunxērunt. Semprōnius Gracchus, cognitō
ad Ītaliam Hannibalis adventū, ex Siciliā exercitum Arīminum traiēcit.

---

11. **Carthāginiēnsibus** – *against the Carthaginians.*
12. **adhūc eā parte inviās** – *as yet, in that region, without roads.*
13. **Trāditur . . . addūxisse** – *He is said to have brought.*
15. **cognitō ad Ītaliam Hannibalis adventū** – *with Hannibal's arrival into
    Italy being learned = when he learned of Hannibal's arrival.*

Hannibal's successes; Fabian tactics

IX. P. Cornēlius Scīpiō Hannibalī prīmus occurrit. Commissō proeliō, fugā-
tīs suīs ipse vulnerātus in castra rediit. Semprōnius Gracchus et ipse conflīgit
apud Trebiam amnem. Is quoque vincitur. Hannibalī multī sē in Ītaliā dēdidērunt. Inde ad Tusciam veniēns Hannibal Flāminiō consulī occurrit. Ipsum   20
Flāminium interēmit; Rōmānōrum XXV mīlia caesa sunt, cēterī diffūgē-
runt. Missus adversus Hannibalem posteā ā Rōmānīs Q. Fabius Maximus.
Is eum differendō pugnam ab impetū frēgit, mox inventā occāsiōne vīcit.

CICERO ON Q. FABIUS MAXIMUS

Though quite old he waged war like a young man, and by his patient
endurance checked the boyish impetuosity of Hannibal. My friend
Ennius admirably speaks of him thus:

One man's delay alone restored our State:
He valued safety more than mob's applause;
Hence now his glory more resplendent grows.

De senectute 4.10, translated by W. A. Falconer

---

17. **Cornēlius Scīpiō . . . prīmus occurrit** – *Scipio was the first to encounter.*
    Commissō proeliō, fugātīs suīs – *after the battle had begun and his forces
    had been routed.* **Suīs** – supply *cōpiīs.*
18. **ipse vulnerātus in castra rediit** – *he himself, having been wounded, re-
    turned to camp.*
20. **Inde ad Tusciam veniēns** – *Coming from there to Etruria.*
23. **Is eum differendō pugnam ab impetū frēgit** – literally, *he broke him from
    his force by delaying battle.* The idea is that Fabius broke Hannibal's
    momentum.
    inventā occāsiōne – *with an opportunity having been found* = *when he had
    found an opportunity.*
    vīcit – supply *eum.*

Battle of Cannae

X. Quingentēsimō et quadrāgēsimō annō ā conditā urbe L. Aemilius Pau-
25 lus P. Terentius Varrō contrā Hannibalem mittuntur Fabiōque succēdunt,
quī abiēns ambō consulēs monuit, ut Hannibalem, callidum et inpatientem ducem, nōn aliter vincerent, quam proelium differendō. Vērum cum
inpatientiā Varrōnis consulis, contrādīcente alterō consule [id est Aemiliō
Paulō], apud vīcum quī Cannae appellātur in Āpūliā pugnātum esset, ambō
30 consulēs ab Hannibale vincuntur. In eā pugnā trīa mīlia Āfrōrum pereunt;
magna pars dē exercitū Hannibalis sauciātur. Nullō tamen Pūnicō bellō
Rōmānī gravius acceptī sunt. Periit enim in eō consul Aemilius Paulus,
consulārēs aut praetōriī XX, senātōrēs captī aut occīsī XXX, nōbilēs virī
CCC, mīlitum XL mīlia, equitum III mīlia et quingentī. In quibus malīs,
35 nēmō tamen Rōmānōrum pācis mentiōnem habēre dignātus est. Servī,
quod numquam ante, manūmissī et mīlitēs factī sunt.

24. **L. Aemilius Paulus P. Terentius Varrō** – supply *et* between the two
names.

26. **quī abiēns** – *who departing,* i.e., when he was leaving office.

ut Hannibalem . . . vincerent – *that they would not defeat Hannibal.*

27. **nōn aliter . . . quam** – *not otherwise than* = *in no other way than.*

proelium differendō – *by delaying battle.*

Vērum – adv., *but.*

cum . . . pugnātum esset – *when it had been fought* = *when a battle had
taken place.*

28. **inpatientiā Varrōnis consulis** – *because of the impatience of the consul
Varro.*

contrādīcente alterō consule – *with the other consul speaking against [it]* =
although the other consul spoke against it.

id est Aemiliō Paulō – *that is Aemilius Paulus.*

32. **gravius acceptī sunt** – *dealt with more severely.*

34. **In quibus malīs** = *et in eīs malīs, and amidst these misfortunes.*

35. **nēmō . . . Rōmānōrum** – *no one of the Romans* = *none of the Romans.*

mentiōnem habēre dignātus est – *stooped to make mention.*

36. **quod numquam ante** – supply *factum erat.*

Livy on the Death of L. Aemilius Paulus in the Battle of Cannae

Gnaeus Lentulus, a tribune of the soldiers, as he rode by on his horse, caught sight of the consul sitting on a stone and covered with blood. "Lucius Aemilius," he cried, "on whom the gods ought to look down in mercy, as the only man without guilt in this day's disaster, take this horse, while you have still a little strength remaining and I can attend you and raise you up and guard you. Make not this battle calamitous by a consul's death; even without that there are tears and grief enough." To this the consul answered, "All honour, Cornelius, to your manhood! But waste not in unavailing pity the little time you have to escape the enemy. Go, and tell the senators in public session to fortify the City of Rome and garrison it strongly before the victorious enemy draws near: in private say to Quintus Fabius that Lucius Aemilius has lived till this hour and now dies remembering his precepts. As for me, let me breathe my last in the midst of my slaughtered soldiers, lest either for a second time I be brought to trial after being consul, or else stand forth the accuser of my colleague, blaming another in defence of my own innocence."

Ab urbe condita 22.49, translated by B. O. Foster

Defection of Italian cities;
Roman prisoners put to death; war in Spain

XI. Post eam pugnam multae Ītaliae cīvitātēs, quae Rōmānīs pāruerant, sē ad Hannibalem transtulērunt. Hannibal Rōmānīs obtulit ut captīvōs redimerent, responsumque est ā senātū eōs cīvēs nōn esse necessāriōs, quī,

37. **quae Rōmānīs pāruerant** – *which had been subject to the Romans.*
38. **obtulit ut captīvōs redimerent** – *offered to the Romans that they [be allowed to] ransom = offered to the Romans to ransom.*
39. **responsumque est ā senātū** – *it was answered by the Senate = the Senate answered.*

Hannibal. Print Collection, Miriam and Ira D. Wallach Division of Art, Prints and Photographs, The New York Public Library, Astor, Lenox, and Tilden Foundations.

cum armātī essent, capī potuissent. Ille omnēs posteā variīs suppliciīs in-   40
terfēcit et trēs modiōs ānulōrum aureōrum Carthāginem mīsit, quōs ex
manibus equitum Rōmānōrum, senātōrum et mīlitum dētrāxerat. Intereā
in Hispāniā, ubi frāter Hannibalis Hasdrubal remanserat cum magnō exercitū, ut eam tōtam Āfrīs subigeret, ā duōbus Scīpiōnibus, Rōmānīs ducibus, vincitur. Perdit in pugnā XXXV mīlia hominum; ex hīs capiuntur X   45
mīlia, occīduntur XXV mīlia. Mittuntur eī ā Carthāginiēnsibus ad reparandās vīrēs XII mīlia peditum, IV mīlia equitum, XX elephantī.

Marcellus engages Hannibal; Macedonian ambassadors captured

XII. Annō quartō postquam ad Ītaliam Hannibal vēnit, M. Claudius Marcellus consul apud Nōlam, cīvitātem Campāniae, contrā Hannibalem bene
pugnāvit. Hannibal multās cīvitātēs Rōmānōrum per Āpūliam, Calabriam,   50
Brittiōs occupāvit. Quō tempore etiam rex Macedoniae Philippus ad eum
lēgātōs mīsit, prōmittēns auxilia contrā Rōmānōs sub hāc condiciōne, ut
dēlētīs Rōmānīs ipse quoque contrā Graecōs ab Hannibale auxilia acciperet.
Captīs igitur lēgātīs Philippī et rē cognitā Rōmānī in Macedoniam M. Vale-
rium Laevīnum īre iussērunt, in Sardiniam T. Manlium Torquātum prōcon-   55
sulem. Nam etiam ea, sollicitāta ab Hannibale, Rōmānōs dēseruerat.

44. **ut eam tōtam Āfrīs subigeret** – *that he might subdue all of her [Hispania]
to the Africans.*

45. **Perdit** – *he lost.*

ex hīs – *from these = out of this number.*

46. **ad reparandās vīrēs** – *to restore his forces.*

50. **per** – *throughout.*

51. **Quō tempore** = *et eō tempore.*

52. **sub hāc condiciōne, ut . . . auxilia acciperet** – *under this condition: that he
should receive help = on the condition that he receive help.*

56. **Nam etiam ea, sollicitāta ab Hannibale** – *For even she [Sardinia], having
been stirred up by Hannibal.*

The Romans simultaneously engage in four wars

XIII. Ita ūnō tempore quattuor locīs pugnābātur: in Ītaliā contrā Hannibalem, in Hispāniīs contrā frātrem ēius Hasdrubalem, in Macedoniā contrā
Philippum, in Sardiniā contrā Sardōs et alterum Hasdrubalem Carthāgi-
60   niēnsem. Is ā T. Manliō prōconsule, quī ad Sardiniam missus fuerat, vīvus
est captus, occīsa cum eō duodecim mīlia, captī mille quingentī, et ā Rōmānīs Sardinia subacta. Manlius victor captīvōs et Hasdrubalem Rōmam
reportāvit. Intereā etiam Philippus ā Laevīnō in Macedoniā vincitur et in
Hispāniā ab Scīpiōnibus Hasdrubal et Māgō, tertius frāter Hannibalis.

Hannibal comes within four miles of Rome; war in Sicily

65   XIV. Decimō annō postquam Hannibal in Ītaliam vēnerat, P. Sulpiciō Cn.
Fulviō consulibus, Hannibal usque ad quartum mīliārium urbis accessit,
equitēs ēius usque ad portam. Mox consulum cum exercitū venientium
metū Hannibal ad Campāniam sē recēpit. In Hispāniā ā frātre ēius Hasdrubale ambō Scīpiōnēs, quī per multōs annōs victōrēs fuerant, interfi-
70   ciuntur, exercitus tamen integer mansit; cāsū enim magis erant quam
virtūte dēceptī. Quō tempore etiam ā consule Marcellō Siciliae magna pars
capta est, quam tenēre Āfrī coeperant, et nōbilissimā urbe Syrācūsānā

57. **pugnābātur** – *the war was being waged.*
60. **Is . . . vīvus est captus** – *he was captured alive.*
61. **occīsa cum eō duodecim mīlia** – *twelve thousand with him were killed.*
    Provide *sunt* with *occīsa* and *captī* in this and the next clause; provide *est*
    with *subacta* in the following clause.
62. **Manlius victor** – *Manlius [being] the victor = victorious Manlius.*
65. **P. Sulpiciō Cn. Fulviō consulibus** – Supply *et* between the two names.
67. **consulum cum exercitū venientium metū** – *from fear of the consuls
    approaching with an army.*
68. **sē recēpit** – *sē recipere, to retreat.*
70. **cāsū** – *by chance.*
    erant . . . dēceptī – *had been entrapped.*
71. **Quō tempore** = *et eō tempore.*

praeda ingēns Rōmam perlāta est. Laevīnus in Macedoniā cum Philippō et multīs Graeciae populīs et rēge Asiae Attalō amīcitiam fēcit, et ad Siciliam profectus Hannōnem quendam, Āfrōrum ducem, apud Agrigentum cīvitā- 75 tem cum ipsō oppidō cēpit; eumque Rōmam cum captīvīs nōbilibus mīsit. XL cīvitātēs in dēditiōnem accēpit, XXVI expugnāvit. Ita omnī Siciliā receptā et Macedoniā fractā, ingentī glōriā Rōmam regressus est. Hannibal in Ītaliā Cn. Fulvium consulem subitō adgressus cum octō mīlibus hominum interfēcit. 80

PLUTARCH ON THE DEATH OF THE MATHEMATICIAN ARCHIMEDES
DURING THE FALL OF SYRACUSE

But what most of all afflicted [the consul] Marcellus was the death of Archimedes. For it chanced that he was by himself, working out some problem with the aid of a diagram, and having fixed his thoughts and his eyes as well upon the matter of his study, he was not aware of the incursion of the Romans or of the capture of the city. Suddenly a soldier came upon him and ordered him to go with him to Marcellus. This Archimedes refused to do until he had worked out his problem and established his demonstration. Whereupon the soldier flew into a passion, drew his sword, and dispatched him. Others, however, say that the Roman came upon him with drawn

74. **amīcitiam** – *an alliance.*

    ad Siciliam profectus – *having set out toward Sicily* = *after he set out toward Sicily.*

76. **cum ipsō oppidō** – *along with the town itself.*

77. **XL cīvitātēs in dēditiōnem accēpit** – *he accepted forty cities into surrender* = *he accepted the surrender of forty cities.*

78. **regressus est** – the unexpressed subject is *he* [i.e., Laevīnus].

    Hannibal in Ītaliā Cn. Fulvium consulem subitō adgressus cum octō mīlibus hominum interfēcit – *Hannibal, when he suddenly attacked the consul Gnaeus Fulvius in Italy, killed [him] along with eight thousand men.*

sword threatening to kill him at once, and that Archimedes, when he saw him, earnestly besought him to wait a little while, that he might not leave the result that he was seeking incomplete and without demonstration; but the soldier paid no heed to him and made an end of him. There is also a third story, that as Archimedes was carrying to Marcellus some of his mathematical instruments, such as sun-dials and spheres and quadrants, by means of which he made the magnitude of the sun appreciable to the eye, some soldiers fell in with him, and thinking that he was carrying gold in the box, slew him. However, it is generally agreed that Marcellus was afflicted at his death, and turned away from his slayer as from a polluted person, and sought out the kindred of Archimedes and paid them honour.

     The Life of Marcellus 19.4–6, translated by Bernadotte Perrin

P. Cornelius Scipio's successes in Spain

XV. Intereā ad Hispāniās, ubi occīsīs duōbus Scīpiōnibus nullus Rōmānus dux erat, P. Cornēlius Scīpiō mittitur, fīlius P. Scīpiōnis, quī ibīdem bellum gesserat, annōs nātus quattuor et vīgintī, vir Rōmānōrum omnium et suā aetāte et posteriōre tempore ferē prīmus. Is Carthāginem Hispāniae capit, in quā omne aurum, argentum et bellī apparātum Āfrī habēbant, nōbi-

85

81. **ubi occīsīs duōbus Scīpiōnibus nullus Rōmānus dux erat** – *where there was no Roman general since the two Scipios had been killed.*

82. **ibīdem** – *in that very place.*

83. **vir Rōmānōrum omnium . . . ferē prīmus** – *a man nearly first of all the Romans.*

     et . . . et – *both . . . and.*

84. **Carthāginem Hispāniae** – *Carthage of Spain*, i.e., Spanish Carthage or *Carthāgo Nova* (modern-day Cartagena).

lissimōs quoque obsidēs, quōs ab Hispānīs accēperant. Māgōnem etiam, frātrem Hannibalis, ibīdem capit, quem Rōmam cum aliīs mittit. Rōmae ingēns laetitia post hunc nuntium fuit. Scīpiō Hispānōrum obsidēs parentibus reddidit; quārē omnēs ferē Hispāniae ūnō animō ad eum transiērunt. Post quae Hasdrubalem, Hannibalis frātrem, victum fugat et praedam 90 maximam capit.

Recapture of Tarentum

XVI. Intereā in Ītaliā consul Q. Fabius Maximus Tarentum recēpit, in quā ingentēs cōpiae Hannibalis erant. Ibi etiam ducem Hannibalis Karthalōnem occīdit, XXV mīlia hominum captīvōrum vendidit, praedam mīlitibus dispertīvit, pecūniam hominum venditōrum ad fiscum retulit. Tum multae 95 cīvitātēs Rōmānōrum, quae ad Hannibalem transierant prius, rursus sē Fabiō Maximō dēdidērunt. Insequentī annō Scīpiō in Hispāniā ēgregiās rēs ēgit et per sē et per frātrem suum L. Scīpiōnem; LXX cīvitātēs recēpērunt. In Ītaliā tamen male pugnātum est. Nam Claudius Marcellus consul ab Hannibale occīsus est. 100

89. **ūnō animō** – *with one mind = unanimously.*

90. **Post quae** = *et post ea, and after these things.*

    Hasdrubalem . . . victum fugat – *he puts to flight Hasdrubal, having been defeated = he defeats and then puts to flight Hasdrubal.*

94. **vendidit** – *i.e., as slaves.*

    mīlitibus – *among his soldiers.*

95. **pecūniam hominum venditōrum** – *money of the men sold = money from the sale of prisoners.*

    fiscum – *the state treasury.*

97. **ēgregiās rēs** – *extraordinary exploits.*

98. **et per sē et per frātrem suum** – compare to *per Hannibalem,* line 2.

    et . . . et – *both . . . and.*

99. **male pugnātum est** – *it was fought badly = the war went badly.*

CICERO ON FABIUS'S RECAPTURE OF TARENTUM

Indeed, with what vigilance, with what skill he recaptured Tarentum! It was in my own hearing that Salinator, who had fled to the
citadel after losing the town, remarked to him in a boasting tone:
"Through my instrumentality, Q. Fabius, you have recaptured Tarentum." "Undoubtedly," said Fabius, laughing, "for if you had not
lost it I should never have recaptured it!"

De senectute 4.11, translated by W. A. Falconer

Further exploits of Scipio in Spain

XVII. Tertiō annō postquam Scīpiō ad Hispāniās [profectus fuerat] rursus
rēs inclitās gerit. Rēgem Hispāniārum magnō proeliō victum in amīcitiam
accēpit et prīmus omnium ā victō obsidēs nōn poposcit.

Hannibal summons Hasdrubal to Italy; Battle of Metaurus

Ind. stat.

XVIII. Despērāns Hannibal Hispāniās contrā Scīpiōnem diūtius posse reti-
105 nērī, frātrem suum Hasdrubalem ad Ītaliam cum omnibus cōpiīs ēvocāvit.

102. **Rēgem Hispāniārum** – *a king of the Spains*, i.e., a king of the Spanish
peninsula.
Rēgem Hispāniārum magnō proeliō victum in amīcitiam accēpit – *he
received a king of the Spains, defeated in a great battle, into an alliance* = *he
defeated a king of the Spains and received him into an alliance.*

103. **prīmus omnium ā victō obsidēs nōn poposcit** – *he, the first of all, did
not demand hostages from the conquered [enemy]* = *he was the first one not
to demand hostages from the conquered enemy.*

104. **Despērāns Hannibal Hispāniās contrā Scīpiōnem diūtius posse retinērī, frātrem suum . . . ēvocāvit** – *Hannibal, giving up hope that the
Spains could be retained any longer against Scipio, recalled his brother.*

Indirect statement

Is veniēns eōdem itinere, quō etiam Hannibal vēnerat, ā consulibus Ap. Claudiō Nerōne et M. Līviō Salīnātōre apud Sēnam, Pīcēnī cīvitātem, in insidiās conpositās incidit. Strēnuē tamen pugnāns occīsus est; ingentēs ēius cōpiae captae aut interfectae sunt, magnum pondus aurī atque argentī Rōmam relātum est. Post haec Hannibal diffīdere iam dē bellī coepit 110 ēventū. Rōmānīs ingēns animus accessit; itaque et ipsī ēvocāvērunt ex Hispāniā P. Cornēlium Scīpiōnem. Is Rōmam cum ingentī glōriā vēnit.

LIVY ON THE DEATH OF HASDRUBAL

Gaius Claudius, the consul, having returned to his camp, ordered the head of Hasdrubal, which he had kept with care and brought with him, to be thrown in front of the enemy's outposts, and that captured Africans should be displayed, as they were, in chains; furthermore that two of them, released from bonds, should go to Hannibal and relate to him what had happened. Hannibal, under the blow of so great a sorrow, at once public and intimate, is reported to have said that he recognized the destiny of Carthage.

Ab urbe condita 27.51, translated by F. G. Moore

• verbs w/ irregular formation / • examples cited
— separated verbs / • translated
— pluperfects / *[~]

106. **ā consulibus . . . in insidiās conpositās incidit** – *he fell into an ambush laid by the consuls.*

108. **Strēnuē tamen pugnāns occīsus est** – *even though he was fighting vigorously, nevertheless he was killed.*

110. **Hannibal diffīdere iam dē bellī coepit ēventū** – *Hannibal now began to doubt the outcome of the war.*

111. **Rōmānīs ingēns animus accessit** – i.e., they were greatly encouraged. (How literally? The subject is *ingēns animus* and the indirect object is *Rōmānīs*.)
    et = *etiam*.

Hace – neuter plural

The cities of Bruttium surrender to the Romans

XIX. Q. Caeciliō L. Valeriō consulibus, omnēs cīvitātēs, quae in Brittiīs ab Hannibale tenēbantur, Rōmānīs sē trādidērunt.

Scipio made consul and sent into Africa; Hannibal recalled from Italy

XX. Annō quartō decimō posteāquam in Ītaliam Hannibal vēnerat, Scīpiō, quī multa bene in Hispāniā ēgerat, consul est factus et in Āfricam missus. Cuī virō dīvīnum quiddam inesse existimābātur, adeō ut putārētur etiam cum nūminibus habēre sermōnem. Is in Āfricā contrā Hannōnem, ducem Āfrōrum, pugnat; exercitum ēius interficit. Secundō proeliō castra capit cum quattuor mīlibus et quingentīs mīlitibus, XI mīlibus occīsīs. Syphā-cem, Numidiae rēgem, quī sē Āfrīs coniunxerat, capit et castra ēius invādit. Syphāx cum nōbilissimīs Numidīs et infīnītīs spoliīs Rōmam ā Scīpiōne mittitur. Quā rē audītā omnis ferē Ītalia Hannibalem dēserit. Ipse ā Car-thāginiēnsibus redīre in Āfricam iubētur, quam Scīpiō vastābat.

The Carthaginians sue for peace

XXI. Ita annō septimō decimō ab Hannibale Ītalia līberāta est. Lēgātī Car-thāginiēnsium pācem ā Scīpiōne petīvērunt; ab eō ad senātum Rōmam missī sunt. Quadrāgintā et quinque diēbus hīs indūtiae datae sunt, quōus-que īre Rōmam et regredī possent; et trīgintā mīlia pondō argentī ab hīs

113. **Q. Caeciliō L. Valeriō consulibus** – supply *et* between the two names.

116. **est** – construe with both *factus* and *missus*.

117. **Cuī virō dīvīnum quiddam inesse existimābātur** – *to which man (= and in this man) there was thought to be something divine.*

   putārētur ... habēre sermōnem – *he was thought to hold conversation(s).*

123. **Quā rē audītā** – *which thing having been heard = and when this thing was heard.*

126. **ab eō** – i.e., by Scipio.

127. **quōusque īre Rōmam et regredī possent** – *until they would be able to go to Rome and return.*

accepta sunt. Senātus ex arbitriō Scīpiōnis pācem iussit cum Carthāginiēnsibus fierī. Scīpiō hīs condiciōnibus dedit: nē amplius quam trīgintā nāvēs 130
habērent, ut quingenta mīlia pondō argentī darent, captīvōs et perfugās
redderent.

Hannibal arrives in Africa

XXII. Interim Hannibale veniente ad Āfricam pāx turbāta est, multa hostīlia ab Āfrīs facta sunt. Lēgātī tamen eōrum ex urbe venientēs ā Rōmānīs
captī sunt, sed iubente Scīpiōne dīmissī. Hannibal quoque frequentibus 135
proeliīs victus ā Scīpiōne petiit etiam ipse pācem. Cum ventum esset ad
colloquium, īsdem condiciōnibus data est, quibus prius additīs quingentīs
mīlibus pondō argentī centum mīlibus lībrārum propter novam perfidiam.
Carthāginiēnsibus condiciōnēs displicuērunt iussēruntque Hannibalem
pugnāre. Infertur ā Scīpiōne et Masinissā, aliō rēge Numidārum, quī amī- 140

129. **ex arbitriō Scīpiōnis** – *on the opinion of Scipio.*

pācem iussit . . . fierī – *ordered peace to be made.*

130. **Scīpiō hīs condiciōnibus dedit** – supply *eam: he gave [it] on these con-*
ditions.

133. **hostīlia** – *hostile acts.*

135. **iubente Scīpiōne** – *with Scipio commanding = on the orders of Scipio.*

136. **petiit** = *petīvit.*

Cum ventum esset ad colloquium – *when it had come to a conference =*
when a conference had been held.

137. **īsdem** = *eīsdem.*

data est – *it was given.*

quibus prius – *with which it was given before = on the same terms it was*
given before.

additīs quingentīs mīlibus pondō argentī centum mīlibus lībrārum –
with a hundred thousand pounds added to the five hundred thousand
pounds of silver.

140. **Infertur . . . bellum** – *war was waged.*

citiam cum Scīpiōne fēcerat, Carthāginī bellum. Hannibal trēs explōrātōrēs
ad Scīpiōnis castra mīsit, quōs captōs Scīpiō circumdūcī per castra iussit
ostendīque hīs tōtum exercitum, mox etiam prandium darī dīmittīque, ut
renuntiārent Hannibalī quae apud Rōmānōs vīdissent.

LIVY ON HANNIBAL'S CONFERENCE WITH SCIPIO

Keeping their armed men at the same distance the generals, each
attended by one interpreter, met, being not only the greatest of their
own age, but equal to any of the kings or commanders of all nations
in all history before their time. For a moment they remained silent,
looking at each other and almost dumbfounded by mutual admira-
tion. Then Hannibal was the first to speak: "If it was foreordained by
fate that I, who was the first to make war upon the Roman people
and who have so often had the victory almost in my grasp, should
come forward to sue for peace, I rejoice that destiny has given me
you, and no one else, to whom I should bring my suit. For you also,
among your many distinctions, it will prove not the least of your
honours that Hannibal, to whom the gods have given the victory
over so many Roman generals, has submitted to you, and that you
have made an end of this war, which was memorable at first for your
disasters and then for ours."

Ab urbe condita 30.30, translated by F. G. Moore

---

141. **Carthāginī** – *against Carthage*
142. **quōs captōs Scīpiō circumdūcī per castra iussit** – *whom Scipio had*
    captured and ordered to be led around the camp.

Battle of Zama

XXIII. Intereā proelium ab utrōque duce instructum est, quāle vix ullā
memoriā fuit, cum perītissimī virī cōpiās suās ad bellum ēdūcerent. Scīpiō
victor recēdit, paene ipsō Hannibale captō, quī prīmum cum multīs equitibus, deinde cum vīgintī, postrēmō cum quattuor ēvāsit. Inventa in castrīs
Hannibalis argentī pondō vīgintī mīlia, aurī octōgintā, cētera supellectilis
cōpiōsa. Post id certāmen, pāx cum Carthāginiēnsibus facta est. Scīpiō
Rōmam rediit, ingentī glōriā triumphāvit atque Āfricānus ex eō appellārī coeptus est. Fīnem accēpit secundum Pūnicum bellum post annum
nōnum decimum, quam coeperat.

[margin: 145 subj cum clause]
[margin: inventa sunt]
[margin: 150]

CASSIUS DIO ON THE BATTLE OF ZAMA

Accordingly, the Romans entered the conflict well marshalled and
eager, but Hannibal and the Carthaginians listless and dejected.
This was owing in part to a total eclipse of the sun; for in view of the

---

145. **proelium . . . instructum est** – *a battle was prepared = preparations were
made for a battle.*

   quāle vix ullā memoriā fuit – *the likes of which there had scarcely been in
any[one's] memory.*

146. **cum perītissimī . . . ēdūcerent** – *since they were the most skillful men to
lead out their forces to war.*

   Scīpiō victor recēdit – *Scipio came away victor.*

149. **cētera supellectilis cōpiōsa** – *other equipment in abundance.*

150. **id certāmen** – *this battle.*

151. **Āfricānus . . . appellārī coeptus est** – *he began to be called Africanus.*

   ex eō – supply *tempore: from that time onward.*

152. **Fīnem accēpit secundum Pūnicum bellum** – literally, *the Second Punic
War received an end.*

   annum nōnum decimum – i.e., eighteen years (see note on *annum
agēns vīcēsimum aetātis,* line 4).

other circumstances, Hannibal suspected that this, too, augured nothing auspicious for them. In this frame of mind they stationed the elephants in front of them as a protection. Suddenly the Romans uttered a great and terrible shout, and smiting their spears against their shields, rushed furiously against the elephants. Thrown into a panic by their charge, most of the beasts did not await their coming, but turned to flight, and receiving frequent wounds caused still greater confusion among those stationed beside them. But some of the beasts charged the Romans, whereupon the latter would stand apart so that they ran through the spaces between the ranks, getting struck with missiles and wounded from close at hand as they passed along. For a time the Carthaginians resisted, but at length, when Masinissa and Laelius fell upon them from the rear with the horsemen, they all fled. The majority of them were destroyed, and Hannibal came very near losing his life. For as he fled, Masinissa pursued him at breakneck speed, giving his horse a free rein. But Hannibal turned, and seeing him thus pursuing, swerved aside slightly and checked his course; thus Masinissa rushed by, and Hannibal got in his rear and wounded him. Thus he made his escape with a few followers.

Roman History 8.14, translated by Earnest Cary

Livy on Hannibal's Speech to the Carthaginian Senate

At Carthage when raising money for the first payment seemed difficult to men whose resources were drained by the long war, and in the Senate House there was mourning and weeping, they say that Hannibal was seen laughing. When Hasdrubal Haedus upbraided him for laughing while the people wept, he being himself the cause of their tears, he said: "If the mind within us could be seen, just as expression of face is seen by our eyes, it would readily be clear to you that this laughter which you upbraid is not that of a happy spirit but of one almost beside itself through misfortunes. Nevertheless it is by no means so untimely as are those senseless, misplaced tears of yours. The time for us to weep was when our arms were taken from us, our ships burned, foreign wars forbidden; for that wound was fatal to us."

Ab urbe condita 30.44, translated by F. G. Moore

qui regnauit añis 23. Quo regnãte: ſedon argiuis meſurus et r
pondeã reppeit. cũ apud hebreos aza ĩ iudea et ieoboa ĩ ihrlm regna
ret. Iſti quoq̃ amulius ſuccedes eis uirnoz filius regnit añis xliiij.
Numitoz pp regis maioz filius: a fre amulio regno pulſus in
agro ſuo uiuit. filia ſua noïe rhea: adimendi party grã: uigo reſ
talis elcã e. q̃ cũ uij patrui ãno geñios edidiſſet infantes: iur
lege in tra uiua defoſſa e. Xm puruulos appe ripam fluñis ex
poſitos fauſtulus regij paſtoz armeti: ao accam lauretiã uro
rem ſuã detulit. q̃ ob pulchzitu³ et rapuitate corpozis gſtuoſi:
lupa a uianis appellabat. vn et ad nram uſq̃ meoziaz metri
cis cellule lupunaia dicuit. Puen cũ adoleuiſſent collcã paſtonus
et latronu maximefecto apud albas amulio: ãiu munitoze in
regno reſtituit De Romulo auctore Romani Imperii
Romanu igit impui: q̃ neq̃ ab exozdio illũ fere min: mz
iaremetis toto ozbe apli humana pot meozia recozdai: a ro
mulo exozdius hz. qui rhee ſiluis: ueſtalis uigis filius, r q̃ptũ puta
tus e mãtis: cũ remo fre uno ptu editus e. Is cũ int paſtozes lat
enaet. xviij añnu natus urbem exiguaz in palatino mõte con
ſtituit xi kl maias: olimpiadis uij anno. et cccc xxiiij. poſt troie
exadiuz: an x añnoz: q̃ decem tribus iſrael a ſennacherib rege cal
deoz naſſeret in mõtes medozu. condita igit ciuitate quã ex ſuo
nomie romaz: a q̃ et romanis nomē inditum e: hec fere a egit.
condito templo: q̃o aſiluz appellauit: pollicitus e cunctis confugieti
bi ipumitatē. quã ob eã multitudinē finitnoz: qui aliq̃ apud
ſuos nues offenſaz cõtraxerat: ad ſe cõfugiētes in ciuitatē recepit.
Latini deniq̃: tuſa q̃ paſtozes: etiaz tranſmarini friges qui ſub e
nea archades: qui ſub euandro duce influxerãt: itaq̃ quaſi ex ba
rijs elementis congregauit corpus unũ. ipiuſq̃ romanũ effecit r.

Page from Renaissance manuscript of the *Breviarium* (ca. 1500). Manuscripts and Archives Division, The New York Public Library, Astor, Lenox, and Tilden Foundations.

Unannotated Latin Text

This section of bare Latin text has been included for use in the classroom. Not having the notes under one's eye in the classroom ensures that the glosses are not used as a crutch and that grammatical concepts have been thoroughly learned. This section is intended for use only after the corresponding passages in the Text and Notes section have been read.

Second Punic War commences; Hannibal lays siege to Saguntum

VII. M. Minuciō Rūfō P. Cornēliō consulibus, bellum Pūnicum secundum Rōmānīs inlātum est per Hannibalem, Carthāginiēnsium ducem, quī Saguntum, Hispāniae cīvitātem Rōmānīs amīcam, obpugnāre adgressus est, annum agēns vīcēsimum aetātis, cōpiīs congregātīs CL mīlium. Huic Rōmānī per lēgātōs dēnuntiāvērunt, ut bellō abstinēret. Is lēgātōs admittere   5
nōluit. Rōmānī etiam Carthāginem mīsērunt, ut mandārētur Hannibalī, nē bellum contrā sociōs populī Rōmānī gereret. Dūra responsa ā Carthāginiēnsibus data sunt. Saguntīnī intereā fame victī sunt, captīque ab Hannibale ultimīs poenīs adficiuntur.

War declared against Carthage; Hannibal crosses the Alps

VIII. Tum P. Cornēlius Scīpiō cum exercitū in Hispāniam profectus est, Ti.   10
Semprōnius in Siciliam; bellum Carthāginiēnsibus indictum est. Hannibal, relictō in Hispāniā frātre Hasdrubale, Pȳrēnaeum transiit. Alpēs, adhūc eā parte inviās, sibi patefēcit. Trāditur ad Ītaliam LXXX mīlia peditum, X mīlia equitum, septem et XXX elephantōs addūxisse. Intereā multī

15 Ligurēs et Gallī Hannibalī sē coniunxērunt. Semprōnius Gracchus, cognitō
ad Ītaliam Hannibalis adventū, ex Siciliā exercitum Arīminum traiēcit.

Hannibal's successes; Fabian tactics

IX. P. Cornēlius Scīpiō Hannibalī prīmus occurrit. Commissō proeliō, fugā-
tīs suīs ipse vulnerātus in castra rediit. Semprōnius Gracchus et ipse conflīgit
apud Trebiam amnem. Is quoque vincitur. Hannibalī multī sē in Ītaliā dēdi-
20 dērunt. Inde ad Tusciam veniēns Hannibal Flāminiō consulī occurrit. Ipsum
Flāminium interēmit; Rōmānōrum XXV mīlia caesa sunt, cēterī diffūgē-
runt. Missus adversus Hannibalem posteā ā Rōmānīs Q. Fabius Maximus.
Is eum differendō pugnam ab impetū frēgit, mox inventā occāsiōne vīcit.

Battle of Cannae

X. Quingentēsimō et quadrāgēsimō annō ā conditā urbe L. Aemilius Pau-
25 lus P. Terentius Varrō contrā Hannibalem mittuntur Fabiōque succēdunt,
quī abiēns ambō consulēs monuit, ut Hannibalem, callidum et inpatientem ducem, nōn aliter vincerent, quam proelium differendō. Vērum cum
inpatientiā Varrōnis consulis, contrādīcente alterō consule [id est Aemiliō
Paulō], apud vīcum quī Cannae appellātur in Āpūliā pugnātum esset, ambō
30 consulēs ab Hannibale vincuntur. In eā pugnā trīa mīlia Āfrōrum pereunt;
magna pars dē exercitū Hannibalis sauciātur. Nullō tamen Pūnicō bellō
Rōmānī gravius acceptī sunt. Periit enim in eō consul Aemilius Paulus,
consulārēs aut praetōriī XX, senātōrēs captī aut occīsī XXX, nōbilēs virī
CCC, mīlitum XL mīlia, equitum III mīlia et quingentī. In quibus malīs,
35 nēmō tamen Rōmānōrum pācis mentiōnem habēre dignātus est. Servī,
quod numquam ante, manūmissī et mīlitēs factī sunt.

Defection of Italian cities; Roman prisoners put to death; war in Spain

XI. Post eam pugnam multae Ītaliae cīvitātēs, quae Rōmānīs pāruerant, sē
ad Hannibalem transtulērunt. Hannibal Rōmānīs obtulit ut captīvōs redimerent, responsumque est ā senātū eōs cīvēs nōn esse necessāriōs, quī,

Joseph Mallord William Turner, *Hannibal Crossing the Alps*, engraved by J. Cousen. Published 1859–61. Photo credit: Tate, London / Art Resource, NY.

cum armātī essent, capī potuissent. Ille omnēs posteā variīs suppliciīs in- 40
terfēcit et trēs modiōs ānulōrum aureōrum Carthāginem mīsit, quōs ex
manibus equitum Rōmānōrum, senātōrum et mīlitum dētrāxerat. Intereā
in Hispāniā, ubi frāter Hannibalis Hasdrubal remanserat cum magnō exercitū, ut eam tōtam Āfrīs subigeret, ā duōbus Scīpiōnibus, Rōmānīs ducibus, vincitur. Perdit in pugnā XXXV mīlia hominum; ex hīs capiuntur X 45
mīlia, occīduntur XXV mīlia. Mittuntur eī ā Carthāginiēnsibus ad reparandās vīrēs XII mīlia peditum, IV mīlia equitum, XX elephantī.

Marcellus engages Hannibal; Macedonian ambassadors captured

XII. Annō quartō postquam ad Ītaliam Hannibal vēnit, M. Claudius Marcellus consul apud Nōlam, cīvitātem Campāniae, contrā Hannibalem bene
pugnāvit. Hannibal multās cīvitātēs Rōmānōrum per Āpūliam, Calabriam, 50

Brittiōs occupāvit. Quō tempore etiam rex Macedoniae Philippus ad eum lēgātōs mīsit, prōmittēns auxilia contrā Rōmānōs sub hāc condiciōne, ut dēlētīs Rōmānīs ipse quoque contrā Graecōs ab Hannibale auxilia acciperet. Captīs igitur lēgātīs Philippī et rē cognitā Rōmānī in Macedoniam M. Vale-
55 rium Laevīnum īre iussērunt, in Sardiniam T. Manlium Torquātum prōconsulem. Nam etiam ea, sollicitāta ab Hannibale, Rōmānōs dēseruerat.

The Romans simultaneously engage in four wars

XIII. Ita ūnō tempore quattuor locīs pugnābātur: in Ītaliā contrā Hannibalem, in Hispāniīs contrā frātrem ēius Hasdrubalem, in Macedoniā contrā Philippum, in Sardiniā contrā Sardōs et alterum Hasdrubalem Carthāgi-
60 niēnsem. Is ā T. Manliō prōconsule, quī ad Sardiniam missus fuerat, vīvus est captus, occīsa cum eō duodecim mīlia, captī mille quingentī, et ā Rōmānīs Sardinia subacta. Manlius victor captīvōs et Hasdrubalem Rōmam reportāvit. Intereā etiam Philippus ā Laevīnō in Macedoniā vincitur et in Hispāniā ab Scīpiōnibus Hasdrubal et Māgō, tertius frāter Hannibalis.

Hannibal comes within four miles of Rome; war in Sicily

65 XIV. Decimō annō postquam Hannibal in Ītaliam vēnerat, P. Sulpiciō Cn. Fulviō consulibus, Hannibal usque ad quartum mīliārium urbis accessit, equitēs ēius usque ad portam. Mox consulum cum exercitū venientium metū Hannibal ad Campāniam sē recēpit. In Hispāniā ā frātre ēius Hasdrubale ambō Scīpiōnēs, quī per multōs annōs victōrēs fuerant, interfi-
70 ciuntur, exercitus tamen integer mansit; cāsū enim magis erant quam virtūte dēceptī. Quō tempore etiam ā consule Marcellō Siciliae magna pars capta est, quam tenēre Āfrī coeperant, et nōbilissimā urbe Syrācūsānā praeda ingēns Rōmam perlāta est. Laevīnus in Macedoniā cum Philippō et multīs Graeciae populīs et rēge Asiae Attalō amīcitiam fēcit, et ad Siciliam
75 profectus Hannōnem quendam, Āfrōrum ducem, apud Agrigentum cīvitātem cum ipsō oppidō cēpit; eumque Rōmam cum captīvīs nōbilibus mīsit. XL cīvitātēs in dēditiōnem accēpit, XXVI expugnāvit. Ita omnī Siciliā receptā et Macedoniā frāctā, ingentī glōriā Rōmam regressus est. Hannibal in

Ītaliā Cn. Fulvium consulem subitō adgressus cum octō mīlibus hominum
interfēcit.   80

P. Cornelius Scipio's successes in Spain

XV. Intereā ad Hispāniās, ubi occīsīs duōbus Scīpiōnibus nullus Rōmānus
dux erat, P. Cornēlius Scīpiō mittitur, fīlius P. Scīpiōnis, quī ibīdem bellum
gesserat, annōs nātus quattuor et vīgintī, vir Rōmānōrum omnium et suā
aetāte et posteriōre tempore ferē prīmus. Is Carthāginem Hispāniae capit,
in quā omne aurum, argentum et bellī apparātum Āfrī habēbant, nōbi-   85
lissimōs quoque obsidēs, quōs ab Hispānīs accēperant. Māgōnem etiam,
frātrem Hannibalis, ibīdem capit, quem Rōmam cum aliīs mittit. Rōmae
ingēns laetitia post hunc nuntium fuit. Scīpiō Hispānōrum obsidēs parentibus reddidit; quārē omnēs ferē Hispāniae ūnō animō ad eum transiērunt.
Post quae Hasdrubalem, Hannibalis frātrem, victum fugat et praedam   90
maximam capit.

Recapture of Tarentum

XVI. Intereā in Ītaliā consul Q. Fabius Maximus Tarentum recēpit, in quā
ingentēs cōpiae Hannibalis erant. Ibi etiam ducem Hannibalis Karthalōnem occīdit, XXV mīlia hominum captīvōrum vendidit, praedam mīlitibus
dispertīvit, pecūniam hominum venditōrum ad fiscum retulit. Tum multae 95
cīvitātēs Rōmānōrum, quae ad Hannibalem transierant prius, rursus sē
Fabiō Maximō dēdidērunt. Insequentī annō Scīpiō in Hispāniā ēgregiās rēs
ēgit et per sē et per frātrem suum L. Scīpiōnem; LXX cīvitātēs recēpērunt.
In Ītaliā tamen male pugnātum est. Nam Claudius Marcellus consul ab
Hannibale occīsus est.   100

Further exploits of Scipio in Spain

XVII. Tertiō annō postquam Scīpiō ad Hispāniās profectus fuerat, rursus
rēs inclitās gerit. Rēgem Hispāniārum magnō proeliō victum in amīcitiam
accēpit et prīmus omnium ā victō obsidēs nōn poposcit.

Hannibal summons Hasdrubal to Italy; Battle of Metaurus

XVIII. Despērāns Hannibal Hispāniās contrā Scīpiōnem diūtius posse reti-
105 nērī, frātrem suum Hasdrubalem ad Ītaliam cum omnibus cōpiīs ēvocāvit.
Is veniēns eōdem itinere, quō etiam Hannibal vēnerat, ā consulibus Ap.
Claudiō Nerōne et M. Līviō Salīnātōre apud Sēnam, Pīcēnī cīvitātem, in
insidiās conpositās incidit. Strēnuē tamen pugnāns occīsus est; ingentēs
ēius cōpiae captae aut interfectae sunt, magnum pondus aurī atque ar-
110 gentī Rōmam relātum est. Post haec Hannibal diffīdere iam dē bellī coepit
ēventū. Rōmānīs ingēns animus accessit; itaque et ipsī ēvocāvērunt ex
Hispāniā P. Cornēlium Scīpiōnem. Is Rōmam cum ingentī glōriā vēnit.

The cities of Bruttium surrender to the Romans

XIX. Q. Caeciliō L. Valeriō consulibus omnēs cīvitātēs, quae in Brittiīs ab
Hannibale tenēbantur, Rōmānīs sē trādidērunt.

Scipio made consul and sent into Africa; Hannibal recalled from Italy

115 XX. Annō quartō decimō posteāquam in Ītaliam Hannibal vēnerat, Scīpiō,
quī multa bene in Hispāniā ēgerat, consul est factus et in Āfricam missus.
Cuī virō dīvīnum quiddam inesse existimābātur, adeō ut putārētur etiam
cum nūminibus habēre sermōnem. Is in Āfricā contrā Hannōnem, ducem
Āfrōrum, pugnat; exercitum ēius interficit. Secundō proeliō castra capit
120 cum quattuor mīlibus et quingentīs mīlitibus, XI mīlibus occīsīs. Syphā-
cem, Numidiae rēgem, quī sē Āfrīs coniunxerat, capit et castra ēius invādit.
Syphāx cum nōbilissimīs Numidīs et infīnītīs spoliīs Rōmam ā Scīpiōne
mittitur. Quā rē audītā omnis ferē Ītalia Hannibalem dēserit. Ipse ā Carthāginiēnsibus redīre in Āfricam iubētur, quam Scīpiō vastābat.

The Carthaginians sue for peace

125 XXI. Ita annō septimō decimō ab Hannibale Ītalia līberāta est. Lēgātī Carthāginiēnsium pācem ā Scīpiōne petīvērunt; ab eō ad senātum Rōmam

missī sunt. Quadrāgintā et quinque diēbus hīs indūtiae datae sunt, quōus-
que īre Rōmam et regredī possent; et trīgintā mīlia pondō argentī ab hīs
accepta sunt. Senātus ex arbitriō Scīpiōnis pācem iussit cum Carthāginiēnsibus fierī. Scīpiō hīs condiciōnibus dedit: nē amplius quam trīgintā nāvēs   130
habērent, ut quingenta mīlia pondō argentī darent, captīvōs et perfugās
redderent.

Hannibal arrives in Africa

XXII. Interim Hannibale veniente ad Āfricam pāx turbāta est, multa hostīlia ab Āfrīs facta sunt. Lēgātī tamen eōrum ex urbe venientēs ā Rōmānīs
captī sunt, sed iubente Scīpiōne dīmissī. Hannibal quoque frequentibus   135
proeliīs victus ā Scīpiōne petiit etiam ipse pācem. Cum ventum esset ad
colloquium, īsdem condiciōnibus data est, quibus prius, additīs quingentīs
mīlibus pondō argentī centum mīlibus lībrārum propter novam perfidiam.
Carthāginiēnsibus condiciōnēs displicuērunt iussēruntque Hannibalem
pugnāre. Infertur ā Scīpiōne et Masinissā, aliō rēge Numidārum, quī amī-   140
citiam cum Scīpiōne fēcerat, Carthāginī bellum. Hannibal trēs explōrātōrēs
ad Scīpiōnis castra mīsit, quōs captōs Scīpiō circumdūcī per castra iussit
ostendīque hīs tōtum exercitum, mox etiam prandium darī dīmittīque, ut
renuntiārent Hannibalī quae apud Rōmānōs vīdissent.

Battle of Zama

XXIII. Intereā proelium ab utrōque duce instructum est, quāle vix ullā   145
memoriā fuit, cum perītissimī virī cōpiās suās ad bellum ēdūcerent. Scīpiō
victor recēdit, paene ipsō Hannibale captō, quī prīmum cum multīs equitibus, deinde cum vīgintī, postrēmō cum quattuor ēvāsit. Inventa in castrīs
Hannibalis argentī pondō vīgintī mīlia, aurī octōgintā, cētera supellectilis
cōpiōsa. Post id certāmen, pāx cum Carthāginiēnsibus facta est. Scīpiō   150
Rōmam rediit, ingentī glōriā triumphāvit atque Āfricānus ex eō appellārī coeptus est. Fīnem accēpit secundum Pūnicum bellum post annum
nōnum decimum, quam coeperat.

COMMENTARY

This section contains a running commentary on the grammar and syntax of Book III of the *Breviarium* as well as additional historical information about the Second Punic War (set off in boxes, for easy reference). These notes need not be read in their entirety, but may be referred to on an as-needed basis. Abbreviated cross-references are to the following commonly used U.S. textbooks:

A&G   *Allen and Greenough's New Latin Grammar* (New Rochelle, N.Y.: Aristide D. Caratzas, 1983) [reprint of 1903 edition]. Available on-line from the Perseus Digital Library at www.perseus.tufts.edu.

ER   *Ecce Romani II,* 3rd Edition (Upper Saddle River, N.J.: Prentice Hall, 2000).

J   *Jenney's Second Year Latin* (Upper Saddle River, N.J.: Prentice Hall, 1990).

LFA   *Latin for Americans,* Level 2 (New York: Glencoe/McGraw-Hill, 2004).

M&F   *Latin: An Intensive Course,* by Floyd L. Moreland and Rita M. Fleischer (Berkeley: University of California Press, 1977).

W   *Wheelock's Latin,* 6th Edition, Revised (New York: Harper Collins, 2005).

Chapter VII

1. **M. Minuciō Rūfō P. Cornēliō consulibus** – Eutropius begins this section of the *Breviarium* by identifying the consular year—the regular

method by which the Romans established the date (cf. lines 24 and 48 and see notes).

The clause is *ablative absolute*. Since classical Latin lacks the present participle of *sum esse*, two nouns, or a noun and and adjective, in the ablative case can function as an *ablative absolute* (W 156, M&F 163, ER 349, LFA 33, J 29, A&G 419a).

Roman *praenomina* were almost always written in abbreviated form (*M., P.,* etc.) except when they appeared alone.

Eutropius here dates the beginning of the Second Punic War to 221 BCE. This was actually the year that Hannibal assumed command of the Carthaginian forces in Spain. He did not besiege Saguntum until 219 and war was not declared by Rome until 218.

---

2. **Rōmānīs** – plural *substantive* (that is, an adjective used in place of a noun) from *Rōmānus, -a, -um* (W 27, M&F 10, ER 349, A&G 288). Other common substantives used in Book III of the *Breviarium* are *Āfrī, Carthāginiēnsēs, Gallī,* and *Graecī*.

inlātum est – perfect passive of *inferō, -ferre*. *Bellum Pūnicum* is the nominative subject, *Rōmānīs* the *dative of indirect object*.

per Hannibalem – The *personal agent* is often expressed by *per* with the accusative (LFA 33, A&G 405b).

Hannibal is regarded by many as one of the greatest generals in history. He was born in 247 BCE; his father was Hamilcar Barca, the commander of the Carthaginian forces in the First Punic War. The Roman historical tradition relates that when Hannibal was nine years old, his father took him on a military expedition into Spain, and made him swear on the altar of Zeus undying hostility to Rome. See illustration, page 2.

Carthāginiēnsium ducem – in apposition to *Hannibalem* (W 19, M&F 363, LFA 8, A&G 282). *Carthāginiēnsium* is a plural *substantive* from *Carthāginiēnsis, -e* (cf. *Rōmānīs*, above). What case does the *-ium* ending indicate in third declension adjectives?

quī Saguntum . . . obpugnāre adgressus est – *relative clause* (W 110, M&F 114, ER 358, LFA 39, A&G 279a). The antecedent of *quī* is *Hannibalem*. The English word order would be *quī adgressus est obpugnāre Saguntum civitātem Hispāniae amīcam Rōmānīs*.

3. **adgressus est** – *deponent verb* (W 234, M&F 176, ER 351, LFA 110, A&G 190). Translate with an *active* meaning: *began*.

> Saguntum was south of the river Ebro and within the limit of Carthaginian influence established by previous treaty. As Eutropius points out, however, Saguntum was allied to Rome, and Hannibal must have expected a Roman response.

4. **agēns** – present participle from *agō, -ere*, modifying *quī* and governing a direct object, *annum vīcēsimum aetātis*.

aetātis – What is the case? Note the short *-is* ending.

> The Romans counted the birth year and the current year inclusively, so the twentieth year of his age means age nineteen. Eutropius gets Hannibal's age wrong: he was twenty-five when he assumed command of the Carthaginian forces in Spain.

cōpiīs congregātīs CL mīlium – *ablative absolute* (W 155, M&F 162, ER 348, LFA 33, J 29, A&G 419). When rendering into English, it is often best to convert the participial phrase to a clause with a finite verb, and choose an appropriate conjunction, such as *when, since, although,* or *after* (e.g., *after he had gathered together a hundred and fifty thousand troops* instead of the more literal *a hundred and fifty thousand troops having been* *gathered together*). The active voice here also makes slightly better English, even though the Latin is passive. **congregātīs** – perfect passive participle of *congregō, -āre.*

Huic – *dative with special verbs* (W 246, M&F 218, ER 343, LFA 155, J 41, A&G 563a). Render into English as if it were the *direct object* of a regular *transitive verb* (*ordered him* instead of *brought orders to him*).

5. **ut bellō abstinēret** – *jussive noun clause (indirect command)* (W 253, M&F 52, ER 363, LFA 135, J 78, A&G 563). Many verbs that mean *to admonish, command*, etc., are followed by *ut* plus the subjunctive. These clauses can be distinguished from *purpose clauses* (W 189, M&F 50, ER 362, LFA 77, J 68, A&G 529 ff.) by the fact that they convey an order, request, or advice of some kind. Render into English with an infinitive: *to abstain from war*, instead of the more literal *that he should abstain from war*. (Reserve use of the English auxiliaries *may* or *might* for *purpose clauses*. For a sentence that contains both a *purpose clause* and a *jussive noun clause* see line 6, below, and note the differences in translation.)

bellō – *ablative of separation* (W 130, M&F 102, ER 348, LFA 214, J 419, A&G 400 ff.). Verbs that mean *to remove, set free, be absent, deprive*, and *lack* usually take an ablative of separation.

abstinēret – The imperfect subjunctive here indicates an action that is to follow the historical main verb *dēnuntiāvērunt*. (The imperfect subjunctive in historical sequence of tenses may indicate action *at the same time* or *after*.) (W 205, M&F 51, ER 363, LFA 102, J 427, A&G 482 ff.).

6. **Rōmānī etiam Carthāginem mīsērunt** – Take *Carthāginem* as an *accusative of place to which without a preposition* (W 262, M&F 372, ER 345, LFA 204, J 418, A&G 427), with an understood direct object, such as *postulātiōnēs: the Romans also sent [demands] to Carthage.*

ut mandārētur Hannibalī – *purpose clause* (W 189, M&F 50, ER 362, LFA 77, J 68, A&G 529 ff.). Verbs that govern the dative in the active voice are used *impersonally* in the passive and the dative is retained (LFA 496, M&F 219, A&G 372). Render into English as though Hannibal were the *subject* of the passive verb: *that Hannibal might be commanded*, rather than the more literal *that it might be commanded to Hannibal.*

This construction is the passive equivalent of *Huic . . . dēnuntiāvērunt* in line 4, above.

7. **nē bellum . . . gereret** – *jussive noun clause* (W 253, M&F 52, ER 363, LFA 135, J 78, A&G 563): *that he should not wage war.* Render into English with an infinitive: *not to make war.*

   ā Carthāginiēnsibus – *ablative of personal agent* with a passive verb (W 118, M&F 65, ER 346, LFA 33, J 420, A&G 405).

8. **data sunt** – perfect passive of *dō, dāre.*

   fame – *ablative of means or instrument* (W 91, M&F 50, ER 346, LFA 20, J 420, A&G 409).

   victī sunt – perfect passive of *vincō, -ere.*

   captīque – perfect passive participle of *capiō, -ere,* here used as a substantive (W 27, M&F 10, ER 349, A&G 288): *the captives.* It is the subject of the passive verb *adficiuntur.*

9. **ultimīs poenīs** – *ablative of means or instrument.* The ultimate punishment is, of course, death.

   adficiuntur – *historical present* (ER 23, LFA 501, A&G 469). In lively narration, the present tense can be used to convey a past action.

Chapter VIII

10. **profectus est** – perfect of deponent *proficiscor;* translate with an active meaning (*set out*) and construe both with *P. Cornēlius Scīpiō in Hispāniam* and *Ti. Semprōnius in Siciliam.* The omission of a word or words necessary to complete the sense—here a verb for the second clause—is called *ellipsis* (M&F 14, A&G 640).

11. **Carthāginiēnsibus** – *dative of reference* (W 270, M&F 367, LFA 155, J 416, A&G 376–377). The dative case often denotes the person or thing to whom a statement refers, for whom it is true, or to whom it is of special interest. It may also denote—as here—the person for whose advantage or disadvantage an action is performed. The latter usage is also called the *dative of advantage or disadvantage.*

12. **relictō in Hispāniā frātre Hasdrubale** – *ablative absolute* (W 155, M&F 162, ER 348, LFA 33, J 29, A&G 419). See note on *cōpiīs congregātīs CL mīlium,* line 4. **relictō** – perfect passive participle of *relinquō, -ere.*

adhūc eā parte inviās – *Inviās* is modifying *Alpēs.* Render into English as a relative clause: *which were as yet.* **eā parte** – *ablative of place where* (W 142, M&F 377, ER 344, LFA 7, J 42, A&G 426). *Parte,* and several other Latin words, are used in this construction without the preposition *in* (LFA 7, A&G 429).

> The exact Alpine pass by which Hannibal entered Italy has been the subject of intense speculation. For a recent treatment of the subject, see *Hannibal Crosses the Alps: The Enigma Re-Examined* by John Prevas (New York: Perseus Books Group, 1998). See Appendix B, Hannibal's route of invasion.

13. **sibi** – *dative of reference* (W 270, M&F 367, LFA 155, J 416, A&G 376).

Trāditur . . . addūxisse – *indirect discourse: personal construction with passive verbs of saying* (A&G 582). This can be recognized as the *personal construction (he is said to have brought)* rather than the *impersonal construction (it is said that he brought)* for two reasons: the *personal construction* is more common with verbs in the present and imperfect tenses, and the *impersonal construction* would normally require an *expressed* accusative subject (e.g., *eum*), which is lacking in this sentence. The perfect infinitive here is used to convey past time.

> 14. **septem et XXX elephantōs** – The famed elephants Hannibal brought with him over the Alps were a smaller African subspecies gathered from the forests at the foot of the Atlas Mountains. They were used effectively against the Romans in the first battles of the war, but most of the herd died during their first winter in Italy. It was not until the final battle of the war—seventeen years

---

later in Africa—that the Carthaginians again used elephants in
large numbers against the Romans. At that time, however, their
effectiveness in battle was minimized by the Romans' simply
breaking lanes in their ranks. For more information, see the
entry for Elephants in the *Oxford Classical Dictionary*, 3rd edition
(New York: Oxford University Press, 1996).

---

15. **cognitō ad Ītaliam Hannibalis adventū** – *ablative absolute* (W 155, M&F
    162, ER 348, LFA 33, J 29, A&G 419). See note on *cōpiīs congregātīs CL
    mīlium*, line 4. **cognitō** – perfect passive participle of *cognōscō, -ere.*

16. **Arīminum** – *accusative of place to which:* no preposition is used with the
    names of cities (W 262, M&F 372, ER 345, LFA 204, J 418, A&G 427).

Chapter IX

P. Cornēlius Scīpiō Hannibalī prīmus occurrit – The battle took
place in autumn 218 at the river Ticinus in northern Italy.

---

17. **Hannibalī** – *dative with a compound verb* (W 247, M&F 220, ER 343,
    LFA 173, J 41, A&G 370). Often the dative appears to function as the
    object of the prepositional prefix (here, the *ob* from *ob + currō*), though
    the preposition would take another case if separate from the verb.

    occurrit – may be either present or perfect. Since the following verb,
    rediit, is perfect, *occurrit* may also be taken as perfect. Since the sen-
    tence after that, however, begins a brief section of *historical present* (ER
    23, LFA 501, A&G 469), we may rather want to take *occurrit* as present.

    Commissō proeliō, fugātīs suīs – two *ablatives absolute* (W 155, M&F
    162, ER 348, LFA 33, J 29, A&G 419). **Commissō** – perfect passive
    participle of *committō.* **fugātīs** – perfect passive participle of *fugō, -āre,*

to put to flight (not *fugiō, -ere,* to flee). **suīs** – Possessive pronouns and adjectives are often used substantively to denote one's own men, troops, forces, etc. (A&G 302d).

18. **ipse vulnerātus in castra rediit** – Latin often employs a perfect participle where English would use a subordinate clause (A&G 496). Render into English as *after he had been wounded, he returned to camp,* instead of the more literal *he himself, having been wounded, returned to camp.* **in castra** – *accusative of place to which* (W 262, M&F 372, ER 345, LFA 204, J 418, A&G 426). Notice how much information this sentence conveys in so few words.

> Scipio's eighteen-year-old son—also named P. Cornelius Scipio—was present at the battle of Ticinus and was said to have saved his wounded father from the battlefield. The son was to be the eventual conqueror of Hannibal and was later conferred the name Africanus.

conflīgit – *historical present* (ER 23, LFA 501, A&G 469). Some manuscripts have *conflixit.*

19. **Hannibalī multī sē in Ītaliā dēdidērunt** – The English word order would be *multī dēdidērunt sē Hannibalī in Ītaliā.* **sē** – third person reflexive pronoun, masculine accusative plural. The gender and number are determined by the subject.

> 20. **Inde ad Tusciam veniēns** – The battle took place in 217 near Lake Trasimene. See Appendix B: Maps and Battle Plans.

Flāminiō consulī – *dative with a compound verb* (W 247, M&F 220, ER 343, LFA 173, J 41, A&G 370). See note on *Hannibalī,* line 17.

21. **Rōmānōrum** – *partitive genitive* (W 98, M&F 154, ER 342, LFA 25, J 414, A&G 346).

caesa sunt – perfect passive of *caedō, -ere.*

22. **Missus** – perfect passive participle of *mittō;* supply *est* and construe with *Q. Fabius Maximus.*

    ā Rōmānīs – *ablative of personal agent* (W 118, M&F 65, ER 346, LFA 33, J 420, A&G 405).

> **Q. Fabius Maximus** – Quintus Fabius Maximus was named dictator —an extraordinary political office employed during military or political crises—in 217 BCE, after the disastrous battle of Lake Trasimene. By pursuing a policy of attrition and avoiding a general engagement with Hannibal's army, he earned the somewhat disparaging name Cunctator, "the Delayer."

---

23. **Is eum differendō pugnam ab impetū frēgit** – The English word order would be *Is frēgit eum ab impetū differendō pugnam.* **Differendō** is a gerund (W 276, M&F 265, ER 356, LFA 141, J 39, A&G 507); it functions in the sentence as an *ablative of means or instrument* (W 91, M&F 50, ER 346, LFA 20, J 420, A&G 409) and takes the object **pugnam**: *by delaying battle.* **Ab impetū** is an *ablative of separation* (W 130, M&F 102, ER 348, LFA 214, J 419, A&G 400 ff.): *from his force.*

    inventā occāsiōne – *ablative absolute* (W 155, M&F 162, ER 348, LFA 33, J 29, A&G 419). See note on *cōpiīs congregātīs CL mīlium,* line 4. **inventā** – pefect passive participle of *inveniō, -īre.*

Chapter X

24. **Quingentēsimō et quadrāgēsimō annō ā conditā urbe** – *ablative of time when* (no preposition is used) (W 99, M&F 116, ER 346, LFA 7, J 422, A&G 423). Giving the number of years since the founding of the city is another regular method by which the Romans established the date (cf. lines 1 and 48).

Eutropius gets the date wrong: the year was 216 BCE, which would have been in the 538th year since the founding of the city. Fabius's term as dictator had expired and there was mounting pressure at Rome to abandon his strategy of exhaustion.

L. Aemilius Paulus – This Roman family name is often spelled Paullus.

25. **mittuntur** – brief return to *historical present* (ER 23, LFA 501, A&G 469).

Fabiōque – *dative with a compound verb* (W 247, M&F 220, ER 343, LFA 173, J 41, A&G 370). See note on *Hannibalī*, line 17. The enclitic *-que* here, as often, signals a new clause.

26. **quī** – The antecedent is *Fabius*.

ut Hannibalem . . . vincerent – *jussive noun clause* (W 253, M&F 52, ER 363, LFA 135, J 78, A&G 563). The English word order would be *ut vincerent Hannibalem (callidum et inpatientem ducem) nōn aliter quam differendō proelium*.

callidum et inpatientem ducem – in apposition to *Hannibalem* (W 19, M&F 363, LFA 8, A&G 282).

27. **proelium differendō** – gerund governing direct object expressing means (W 276, M&F 266, ER 356, LFA 141, J 39, A&G 507). See note on *differendō pugnam*, line 23.

Vērum cum inpatientiā . . . vincuntur – The core of this sentence is: *cum pugnātum esset . . . ambō consulēs ab Hannibale vincuntur*. The English word order of the entire sentence would be: *vērum cum pugnātum esset apud vīcum in Āpūliā quī appellātur Cannae inpatientiā consulis Varrōnis—alterō consule contrādīcente [id est Aemiliō Paulō]—ambō consulēs vincuntur ab Hannibale*.

cum . . . pugnātum esset – *cum clause (circumstantial)* (W 211, M&F 248, ER 361, LFA 504, J 213, A&G 546). Render *cum* into English as *when* here.

28. **inpatientiā** – *ablative of cause* (W 444, M&F 164, ER 346, LFA 499, J 42, A&G 404). This construction is sometimes difficult to distinguish from the ablative of means or instrument (W 91, M&F 50, ER 346, LFA 20, J 420, A&G 409). **Varrōnis consulis** – What is the case of these two nouns? Note the short *-is* endings.

> The Roman historical tradition laid all of the strategic responsibility for the disaster at Cannae on Varro, the plebeian consul.

contrādīcente alterō consule – *ablative absolute* (W 155, M&F 162, ER 348, LFA 33, J 29, A&G 419). **contrādīcente** – present active participle of *contrādīcō, -ere*. The active form of the participle can also be used to form an ablative absolute.

id est Aemiliō Paulō – This may have originated as a scribal note. It is lacking in some manuscripts.

29. **pugnātum esset** – The *impersonal passive* construction is commonly used with *pugnō* (A&G 208d): *when it had been fought*. Render into English as *when a battle had taken place*. As usual, the subjunctive in the *cum clause* is rendered into English as indicative.

30. **vincuntur** – The narrative is back in *historical present* (ER 23, LFA 501, A&G 469) because of the immediacy of the action.

Āfrōrum – *partitive genitive* (W 98, M&F 154, ER 342, LFA 25, J 414, A&G 346). *Āfrī* is a plural *substantive* (W 27, M&F 10, ER 349, A&G 288) from *Āfer, Āfra, Āfrum* used to mean specifically the Carthaginians or their allies.

Although his forces were greatly outnumbered, Hannibal was able to outflank the Romans in a display of tactical brilliance. The Celtic and Spanish troops Hannibal had presented at his center were easily beaten back by the Roman infantry. The Romans then pursued the retreating enemy past Hannibal's strong African infantry on the wings. When Hannibal's cavalry attacked from the rear, the Roman army was surrounded and completely annihilated. For a detailed account of this battle, see *Cannae: The Experience of Battle in the Second Punic War* by Gregory Daley (New York: Routledge, 2001). See Appendix B: Maps and Battle Plans.

31. **Nullō tamen Pūnicō bellō** – *ablative of time when* (no preposition is used) (W 99, M&F 116, ER 346, LFA 7, J 422, A&G 423). Many expressions use the construction *time when*, where in English the main idea is *place* (A&G 424d).

32. **gravius** – *comparative adverb* (W 219, M&F 153, ER 350, LFA 53, A&G 218).

    acceptī sunt – perfect passive of *accipiō*.

33. **aut** – Eutropius uses *aut* as if it were *vel* (i.e., to introduce a nonexclusive alternative). In classical usage, *aut* introduces an antithesis positively excluding what precedes (i.e., either *consulārēs* or *praetōriī*, not both; either *captī* or *occīsī*, not both, etc.) (cf. A&G 324e).

34. **mīlitum . . . equitum** – *partitive genitives* (W 98, M&F 154, ER 342, LFA 25, J 414, A&G 346).

    In quibus malīs – The relative pronoun *quī, quae, quod* often stands at the beginning of a sentence, serving to connect it with the sentence that precedes (M&F 115, LFA 204, A&G 308f). It may be translated by an English demonstrative (*this/that*) with or without the conjunction *and*: *in these misfortunes* or *and in these misfortunes*.

praetōriī XX . . . equitum III mīlia et quingentī – Eutropius's figures for the devastating Roman losses at Cannae are similar to those given by Livy (which are considered by many to be the most convincing). Polybius put the casualty figure even higher at about seventy thousand dead. By either account, the number of fatalities was likely the highest of any battle in history on a single day.

35. **pācis** – *objective genitive* (W 442, M&F 178, J 41, A&G 347–48).

    mentiōnem habēre – The usual idiom is *mentiōnem facere*.

    dignātus est – perfect of the *deponent verb* (W 234, M&F 176, ER 351, LFA 110, A&G 190), *dignor, -ārī*. Translate with an active meaning: *stooped*.

36. **quod numquam ante [factum erat]** – The relative pronoun *quī, quae, quod* may refer to a group of words or an idea (A&G 307d, note).

    manūmissī et mīlitēs factī sunt – Construe *sunt* with both *manūmissī* and *factī*. **mīlitēs** – *predicate nominative with a passive verb of appointing, making, etc.* (A&G 393a).

The Romans refused to admit defeat: they made every effort to press legionaries into service, including releasing convicts and freeing slaves.

Chapter XI

37. **multae Ītaliae cīvitātēs** – *Ītaliae* is a noun in the genitive case, not an adjective: *many cities of Italy.*

One of Hannibal's principal aims in invading Italy was to weaken Rome permanently by causing her allies to revolt. His crushing victory at Cannae did lead to the defection of much of southern Italy, including Capua (the second-largest city in Italy). However, his strategic aim largely failed, and central Italy and all of the Latin colonies remained loyal to Rome. See Introduction for background to Rome's alliances with its Italian neighbors. See the entry for Rome in the *Oxford Classical Dictionary*, 3rd Edition (New York: Oxford University Press, 1996) for more on Rome's conquest of the Italian peninsula and its relationship with the cities of southern Italy.

Rōmānīs pāruerant – Verbs that mean *to obey* govern the dative case (W 246, M&F 218, LFA 155, J 41, A&G 563a). Normally, render these datives into English as the direct objects of regular transitive verbs (i.e., *had obeyed the Romans;* see note for *Huic Rōmānī . . . dēnuntiāvērunt,* line 4). Here, however, render as *had been subject to the Romans.* The pluperfect here conveys time prior to that of the historical main verb, *transtulērunt.*

38. **transtulērunt** – perfect of *transferō, -ferre.*

   obtulit ut captīvōs redimerent – *jussive noun clause* (W 253, M&F 52, ER 363, LFA 135, J 78, A&G 563). See note on *ut bellō abstinēret,* line 5. **obtulit** – perfect of *offerō, -ferre.*

39. **responsumque est** – perfect passive of *respondeō, -ēre,* used impersonally (A&G 208d): *it was answered.* The enclitic *-que* here signals a new clause.

   ā senātū – *ablative of personal agent* (W 118, M&F 65, ER 346, LFA 33, J 420, A&G 405).

   eōs cīvēs nōn esse necessāriōs – *indirect discourse* (W 164, M&F 100, ER 365, LFA 117, J 139, A&G 577 ff.). When rendering into English, supply *that* and change the infinitive to a finite verb: *that those citizens were not necessary.*

quī . . . capī potuissent – *relative clause of characteristic* (W 269, M&F 234, LFA 504, J 225, A&G 535): *who . . . (were the sort who) had been able to be captured.* **potuissent** – *pluperfect subjunctive.*

40. **cum armātī essent** – *cum clause (adversative)* (W 211, M&F 249, ER 361, LFA 505, J 213, A&G 549). Render *cum* into English as *although* or *while* here. As usual, the subjunctive in the *cum clause* is rendered into English as indicative.

    variīs suppliciīs – *ablative of means or instrument* (W 91, M&F 50, ER 346, LFA 20, J 420, A&G 409).

41. **ānulōrum aureōrum** – *partitive genitive* (W 98, M&F 154, ER 342, LFA 25, J 414, A&G 346).

The gold ring was a military decoration and mark of rank, limited to *nobiles* and *equites.*

Carthāginem – *accusative of place to which:* no preposition is used with the names of cities (W 262, M&F 372, ER 345, LFA 204, J 418, A&G 427).

---

42. **Intereā in Hispāniā** – The narrative now turns to the war in Spain, where the Romans had wisely sent an army to prevent reinforcements from reaching Hannibal.

---

44. **ut eam tōtam Āfrīs subigeret** – *purpose clause* (W 189, M&F 50, ER 362, LFA 77, J 68, A&G 529 ff.). The imperfect subjunctive here denotes action *at the same time as or after* that of the historical main verb, *remanserat* (W 205, M&F 51, ER 362, LFA 102, J 427, A&G 482 ff.). **Āfrīs** – *dative of reference* (W 270, M&F 367, LFA 155, J 416, A&G 376). **eam** – The antecedent is *Hispania.* When a Latin pronoun stands for a noun that is grammatically masculine or feminine, but which has no actual sex, it is usually best to translate as *it: all of her = all of it.* (Note,

however, that the glosses at the bottom of the text here and at line 56 translate the gender literally to better show the syntactical relationships.)

ā duōbus Scīpiōnibus – *ablative of personal agent* with a passive verb (W 118, M&F 65, ER 346, LFA 33, J 420, A&G 405).

45. **vincitur** – another brief section of *historical present* (ER 23, LFA 501, A&G 469) begins here.

> The two Scipios were P. Cornelius and Gnaeus, the father and uncle of P. Scipio Africanus.

46. **eī** – *indirect object;* masculine dative singular of *is, ea, id.*

ā Carthāginiēnsibus – *ablative of personal agent* with a passive verb (W 118, M&F 65, ER 346, LFA 33, J 420, A&G 405).

ad reparandās vīrēs – accusative *gerundive* after the preposition *ad* to indicate *purpose* (W 278, M&F 266, LFA 142, J 42, A&G 506): *to restore his forces* (literally, *for the purpose of his forces to be restored*). **vīrēs** – plural of *vīs, vīs: forces* (not *vir, virī: men*).

Chapter XII

48. **Annō quartō** – *ablative of time when* (no preposition is used) (W 99, M&F 116, ER 346, LFA 7, J 422, A&G 423). Giving the number of years since Hannibal's arrival in Italy is another method Eutropius uses in Book III of the *Breviarium* to establish the date (cf. lines 1 and 24).

> 49. **apud Nōlam** – Nola was a Campanian hinterland town, which had resisted Hannibal, even though Capua and much of southern Italy had defected to the Carthaginian side. Marcellus successfully defended it against three Carthaginian attacks.

51. **Quō tempore** – *ablative of time when* (no preposition is used) (W 99, M&F 116, ER 346, LFA 7, J 422, A&G 423). For **Quō** standing at the beginning of this sentence (M&F 115, LFA 204, A&G 308f), see note on *In quibus malīs*, line 34.

    ad eum – i.e., *ad Hannibalem.*

52. **prōmittēns** – present active participle modifying *Philippus;* it takes the direct (neuter plural) object *auxilia: promising help.*

    ut . . . auxilia acciperet – *jussive noun clause* (W 253, M&F 52, ER 363, LFA 135, J 78, A&G 563) defining *hāc condiciōne.* See note on *ut bellō abstinēret*, line 5.

53. **dēlētīs Rōmānīs** – *ablative absolute* (W 155, M&F 162, ER 348, LFA 33, J 29, A&G 419). See note on *cōpiīs congregātīs CL mīlium*, line 4. **dēlētīs** – perfect passive participle of *dēleō, -ēre.*

54. **Captīs igitur lēgātīs Philippī et rē cognitā** – two *ablatives absolute* (W 155, M&F 162, ER 348, LFA 33, J 29, A&G 419) separated by *et.* **cognitā** – perfect passive participle of *cognōscō, -ere.*

    Rōmānī . . . īre iussērunt . . . T. Manlium Torquātum prōconsulem – *iubeō* takes the *infinitive with subject accusative* (W 254, ER 365, LFA 508, J 78, A&G 563a). *Iussērunt* governs both *M. Valerium Laevīnum* and *T. Manlium Torquātum prōconsulem* (see note on *ellipsis*, line 10). The English word order would be: *Rōmānī iussērunt M. Valerium Laevīnum īre in Macedoniam [et] T. Manlium Torquātum prōconsulem [īre] in Sardiniam.*

---

55. **prōconsulem** – the title under which a consul received governance of a province at the expiration of his term of office. T. Manlius Torquatus had led a successful campaign in Sardinia twenty years earlier as consul. See Appendix C: Roman Magistracies.

---

56. **ea** – the antecedent is *Sardiniam.* See note on *eam*, line 44.

    sollicitāta – perfect passive participle of *sollicitō, -āre.*

dēseruerat – The pluperfect indicative denotes time prior to the perfect verb, *iussērunt*, in the previous sentence.

Chapter XIII

57. **quattuor** – modifies *locīs*. Cardinal numbers from *quattuor* to *centum* do not decline (W 97, ER 326, LFA 45, A&G 133).

    pugnābātur – The *impersonal passive* construction is commonly used with *pugnō* (A&G 208d): *it was being fought*. Render into English as *the war was being waged*. See note for *cum . . . pugnātum esset*, line 29.

---

59. **alterum Hasdrubalem** – known as Hasdrubal the Bald.

---

60. **ā T. Manliō prōconsule** – *ablative of personal agent* (W 118, M&F 65, ER 346, LFA 33, J 420, A&G 405).

    quī – the antecedent is *T. Manliō prōconsule*.

    missus fuerat – *fueram, fuerās*, etc., are sometimes used for *eram, erās*, etc., in the formation of the pluperfect passive (A&G 184, note).

61. **captus** – perfect passive participle of *capiō, -ere*.

    occīsa – perfect passive participle of *occīdō, -ere;* neuter plural because it modifies *mīlia*.

    captī – perfect passive participle of *capiō, -ere*.

62. **subacta** – perfect passive participle of *subigō, -ere*.

63. **ā Laevīnō . . . ab Scīpiōnibus** – *ablatives of personal agent* (W 118, M&F 65, ER 346, LFA 33, J 420, A&G 405).

    vincitur – construe with *Philippus, Hasdrubal,* and *Māgō*. The narrative is back in *historical present*.

Chapter XIV

65. **Decimō annō** – *ablative of time when* (no preposition is used) (W 99, M&F 116, ER 346, LFA 7, J 422, A&G 423).

    P. Sulpiciō Cn. Fulviō consulibus – *ablative absolute.*

> 66. **Hannibal usque ad quartum mīliārium urbis accessit** – 211 BCE. This was an attempt to draw the Roman army away from Capua, which it had been besieging for the last year. The attempt failed: only part of the Roman forces was dispatched to meet Hannibal, and the siege continued.

---

67. **consulum cum exercitū venientium metū** – The English word order would be *metū consulum venientium cum exercitū.* **metū** – *ablative of cause* (W 444, M&F 164, ER 346, LFA 499, J 42, A&G 404). **consulum venientium** – *objective genitives* (W 442, M&F 178, J 41, A&G 347–48).

68. **ā frātre ēius Hasdrubale** – *ablative of personal agent* (W 118, M&F 65, ER 346, LFA 33, J 420, A&G 405).

69. **interficiuntur** – *historical present* (ER 23, LFA 501, A&G 469); the subject is *ambō Scīpiōnēs.*

70. **cāsū enim magis erant quam virtūte dēceptī** – the English word order would be *enim dēceptī erant magis cāsū quam virtūte.* **cāsū . . . virtūte** – *ablatives of means or instrument* (W 91, M&F 50, ER 346, LFA 20, J 420, A&G 409): render *cāsū* here as *by chance.* **erant . . . dēceptī** – pluperfect passive indicative of *dēcipiō: had been entrapped.*

> The two Scipios, along with almost half their men, were killed in 211 BCE in the Tader Valley while marching south from Saguntum, with their forces divided in two. The Romans were able to regroup, though, and defeat the advancing Carthaginians.

71. **Quō tempore** – *ablative of time when* (no preposition is used) (W 99, M&F 116, ER 346, LFA 7, J 422, A&G 423). For **Quō** standing at the beginning of this sentence (M&F 115, LFA 204, A&G 308f), see note on *In quibus malīs,* line 34.

ā consule Marcellō – *ablative of personal agent* (W 118, M&F 65, ER 346, LFA 33, J 420, A&G 405).

Siciliae – *partitive genitive* (W 98, M&F 154, ER 342, LFA 25, J 414, A&G 346).

72. **nōbilissimā urbe Syrācūsānā** – *ablative of separation* (W 130, M&F 102, ER 348, LFA 214, J 419, A&G 400 ff.); *nōbilissimā* is the superlative degree (W 172, M&F 150, ER 65, LFA 52, A&G 124) of the adjective *nōbilis.*

73. **praeda ingēns** – subject of the passive verb *perlāta est.*

Rōmam – *accusative of place to which:* no preposition is used with the names of cities (W 262, M&F 372, ER 345, LFA 204, J 418, A&G 427).

perlāta est – perfect passive of *perferō, -ferre.*

> The mathematician Archimedes was killed by the Romans when Syracuse was taken. It is said that he had been taking part in the defense of the city through the construction of various engines of war. See extract from Plutarch, pages 11–12.

cum . . . rēge Asiae Attalō – *cum* governs three objects: *Philippō, multīs Graeciae populīs,* and *rēge Asiae Attalō.* The genitives *Graeciae* and *Asiae* are placed between the words they modify, as often in Latin.

74. **ad Siciliam profectus . . . cum ipsō oppidō cēpit** – The English word order would be *profectus ad Siciliam cēpit quendam Hannōnem, ducem Āfrōrum, apud cīvitātem Agrigentum cum ipsō oppidō.* **profectus** – perfect participle of the deponent *proficiscor, -ī.* Translate with an active meaning: *having set out.*

76. **cēpit** – perfect of *capiō, -ere.*

Rōmam – *accusative of place to which:* no preposition is used with the names of cities (W 262, M&F 372, ER 345, LFA 204, J 418, A&G 427).

77. **omnī Siciliā receptā et Macedoniā fractā** – two *ablatives absolute* (W 155, M&F 162, ER 348, LFA 33, J 29, A&G 419), separated by *et*. **fractā** – perfect passive participle of *frangō, -ere*.

78. **ingentī glōriā** – *ablative of manner* (W 92, M&F 50, ER 347, LFA 14, A&G 412). The preposition *cum* is ordinarily not used when the ablative is modified by an adjective (compare with *cum ingentī glōriā*, line 112, where *cum* is nevertheless retained).

regressus est – perfect of the *deponent verb* (W 234, M&F 176, ER 351, LFA 110, A&G 190) *regredior, -gredī*. Translate with an active meaning: *he returned.*

Hannibal . . . subitō adgressus . . . interfēcit – The English word order would be *Hannibal, subitō adgressus Cn. Fulvium consulem in Ītaliā, interfēcit [eum] cum octō mīlibus hominum.* For translating the perfect participle, *adgressus,* as a subordinate clause, see note on *ipse vulnerātus in castra rediit,* line 18.

---

79. **consulem** – Eutropius gets Fulvius's title wrong: he was a praetor, not a consul.

---

hominum – *partitive genitive* (W 98, M&F 154, ER 342, LFA 25, J 414, A&G 346).

Chapter XV

81. **Intereā ad Hispāniās . . . ferē prīmus** – The core of this sentence is *Intereā P. Cornēlius Scīpiō mittitur ad Hispāniās.* The English word order of the entire sentence would be: *Intereā P. Cornēlius Scīpiō (fīlius P. Scīpiōnis, quī gesserat bellum ibīdem), nātus quattuor et vīgintī annōs, vir ferē prīmus omnium Rōmānōrum et suā aetāte et posteriōre tempore,*

mittitur ad Hispāniās, ubi nullus Rōmānus dux erat occīsīs duōbus Scī-piōnibus.

occīsīs duōbus Scīpiōnibus – *ablative absolute* (W 155, M&F 162, ER 348, LFA 33, J 29, A&G 419–20). Render into English as *since the two Scipios had been killed.* See note on *cōpiīs congregātīs CL mīlium*, line 4. **occīsīs** – perfect passive participle of *occīdō, -ere.*

82. **mittitur** – *historical present* (ER 23, LFA 501, A&G 469).

    quī – the antecedent is *P. Scīpiōnis* (not *P. Cornēlius Scīpiō*).

83. **annōs nātus quattuor et vīgintī** – *annōs* is an *accusative of duration of time* (W 263, M&F 116, LFA 97, J 418, A&G 423), the normal construction with *nātus*. **nātus** – perfect participle of *nāscor, -ī.*

    vir – in apposition to *P. Cornēlius Scīpiō* (W 19, M&F 363, LFA 8, A&G 282).

    Rōmānōrum omnium – *partitive genitive* (W 98, M&F 154, ER 342, LFA 25, J 414, A&G 346).

    suā aetāte and **posteriōre tempore** – *ablative of time when* (no preposition is used) (W 99, M&F 116, ER 346, LFA 7, J 422, A&G 423).

Scipio is considered one of the greatest of all Roman generals. He had witnessed Hannibal's tactics firsthand at many of the major battles in Italy (including Ticinus—where he is said to have saved his father's life—Trebia, and Cannae). His Spanish campaigns introduced a number of innovations into the Roman military, including the adoption of the Spanish sword and the improvement of the *pilum* (the heavy javelin of the Roman infantry) as well as a number of important tactical reforms.

---

85. **omne** – modifies the next three accusatives. It is neuter because it agrees with the nearest noun (A&G 287). Words that mean *"the whole"* take *a case in agreement* and not the *partitive genitive* (*omne aurum*, not *omne aurī*).

nōbilissimōs quoque obsidēs – second direct object of *capit*. **nōbilissi-mōs** – superlative degree of *nōbilis, -e* (W 172, M&F 150, ER 65, LFA 52, A&G 124).

87. **Rōmam** – *accusative of place to which:* no preposition is used with the names of cities (W 262, M&F 372, ER 345, LFA 204, J 418, A&G 427).

    Rōmae – *locative* (W 262, M&F 103, ER 349, LFA 178, J 423, A&G 427): *in Rome.*

89. **omnēs ferē Hispāniae** – The adverb is placed between the adjective and noun it modifies, as often in Latin.

90. **Post quae** – For the relative pronoun *quī, quae, quod* standing at the beginning of the sentence, see note on *In quibus malīs,* line 34 (M&F 115, LFA 204, A&G 308f).

    Hasdrubalem . . . victum fugat – Latin sometimes employs a perfect participle where English would use a coordinate clause (A&G 496 n. 2). Render into English as *he defeats and then puts to flight Hasdrubal,* instead of the more literal *he puts to flight Hasdrubal, [after Hasdrubal was] defeated.* The narrative is back in *historical present.*

Chapter XVI

94. **hominum cāptīvōrum** – *partitive genitive* (W 98, M&F 154, ER 342, LFA 25, J 414, A&G 346).

95. **venditōrum** – perfect passive participle, genitive plural, of *vendō, -ere.* It modifies the genitive plural *hominum: of the men [who were] sold.*

    retulit – perfect of *referō, -ferre.*

97. **Insequentī annō** – *ablative of time when* (no preposition is used) (W 99, M&F 116, ER 346, LFA 7, J 422, A&G 423). **Insequentī** – ablative singular of present participle from *insequor, -ī.* Present (and future) participles of deponent verbs have *active* forms (W 237, M&F 178, ER 135, LFA 110, J 5, A&G 190a).

99. **pugnātum est** – See note for *cum . . . pugnātum esset,* line 29.

ab Hannibale – *ablative of personal agent* (W 118, M&F 65, ER 346, LFA 33, J 420, A&G 405).

100. **occīsus est** – perfect passive of *occīdō, -ere*.

Chapter XVII

101. **Tertiō annō** – *ablative of time when* (no preposition is used) (W 99, M&F 116, ER 346, LFA 7, J 422, A&G 423).

profectus fuerat – perfect of deponent *proficīscor, -ī*. See note on *missus fuerat*, line 60.

102. **rēs inclitās** – Compare to *ēgregiās rēs*, line 97.

> **Hispāniārum** – The Romans divided Spain into *Hispania Citerior* and *Ulterior*, hence the plural *Hispaniae*.

Rēgem Hispāniārum magnō proeliō victum in amīcitiam accēpit – Render into English as two coordinate clauses (A&G 496 n. 2): *he defeated . . . and he received*. See note on *Hasdrubalem . . . victum fugat*, line 90.

magnō proeliō – *ablative of time when* (no preposition is used) (W 99, M&F 116, ER 346, LFA 7, J 422, A&G 423). See note on *Nullō tamen Pūnicō bellō*, line 31.

103. **poposcit** – perfect of *poscō, -ere*.

> Demanding hostages from a conquered enemy was the normal practice in ancient warfare and not doing so was an overture of good will.

Chapter XVIII

104. **Despērāns Hannibal . . . ēvocāvit** – Latin often employs a present participle where English would use a subordinate clause (A&G 496). See note on *ipse vulnerātus in castra rediit*, line 18. The English word order would be *Hannibal (despērāns Hispāniās posse retinērī diūtius contrā Scīpiōnem) ēvocāvit suum frātrem Hasdrubalem ad Ītaliam cum omnibus cōpiīs.*

   Hispāniās contrā Scīpiōnem diūtius posse retinērī – *indirect discourse* (W 164, M&F 100, ER 365, LFA 117, J 139, A&G 577 ff.) governed by the present participle, *despērāns*. **retinērī** – *passive infinitive*.

106. **Is . . . in insidiās conpositās incidit** – The English word order would be *Is (veniēns eōdem itinere, quō Hannibal etiam vēnerat) incidit in insidiās conpositās ā consulibus Ap. Claudiō Nerōne et M. Līviō Salīnātōre apud Sēnam, Pīcēnī cīvitātem.*

   eōdem itinere – *ablative of place where (way by which)* (W 142, M&F 377, LFA 7, J 42, A&G 429a).

   ā consulibus – Construe with *conpositās.*

---

107. **apud Sēnam** – near the river Metaurus, in 207 BCE. This was one of the most decisive battles of the war. The Romans had been successful up to this point in keeping Hannibal from receiving reinforcements, and it was critical that Hasdrubal's army of more than twenty thousand men be kept from reaching Hannibal in the south. The combined forces of the two consuls (Nero had risked leaving only a part of his forces to guard Hannibal) and the praetor L. Porcius Licinius confronted Hasdrubal in June 207 BCE and annihilated his entire army. It is said that Hasdrubal's severed head was flung into Hannibal's camp.

---

108. **conpositās** – perfect passive participle of *conpōnō, -ere.*

   Strēnuē – adverb modifying the present participle, *pugnāns.*

110. **Rōmam** – *accusative of place to which:* no preposition is used with the names of cities (W 262, M&F 372, ER 345, LFA 204, J 418, A&G 427).

  relātum est – perfect passive of *referō, -ferre.*

  haec – neuter plural.

  Hannibal diffīdere iam dē bellī coepit ēventū – The English word order would be *Hannibal iam coepit diffīdere dē ēventū bellī.*

111. **accessit** – perfect of *accēdō, -ere.*

112. **cum ingentī glōriā** – *ablative of manner* (W 92, M&F 50, ER 347, LFA 14, A&G 412a). *Cum* is ordinarily not used when the ablative is modified by an adjective. As here, though, it is sometimes retained. Compare with *ingentī glōriā,* line 78, where *cum* is not used.

Chapter XIX

113. **Q. Caeciliō L. Valeriō consulibus** – *ablative absolute* (W 155, M&F 162, ER 348, LFA 33, J 29, A&G 419a).

  ab Hannibale – *ablative of personal agent* (W 118, M&F 65, ER 346, LFA 33, J 420, A&G 405).

Chapter XX

116. **ēgerat** – pluperfect of *agō, -ere.*

---

consul est factus et in Āfricam missus – Scipio, in fact, faced significant senatorial opposition (led by Q. Fabius Maximus) to his planned invasion of Africa. He first crossed into Sicily where he trained an army composed mainly of volunteers (including some of the disgraced survivors of the Battle of Cannae). From there he was allowed to launch an offensive on Africa, but without material support from the Senate.

---

  factus – perfect passive participle of *faciō, -ere.*

  missus – perfect passive participle of *mittō, -ere.*

117. **Cuī virō** – For the *dative with a compound verb* (W 247, M&F 220, ER 343, LFA 173, J 41, A&G 370), see note on *Hannibalī*, line 17; for *cuī* standing at the beginning of this sentence (M&F 115, LFA 204, A&G 308f), see note on *In quibus malīs*, line 34.

   quiddam – neuter singular of *quīdam*. When used as a pronoun (*someone, something*), the neuter singular form is *quiddam* instead of *quoddam* (W 174, A&G 151c).

   ut putārētur – *result clause* (W 196, M&F 232, ER 361, LFA 92, A&G 536 ff.). A *result clause* can often be identified by the presence of an adverb such as *adeō* indicating degree: "He did something to such an extent, that he . . ." The imperfect subjunctive is used here to denote action *at the same time* as that of the historical main verb, *existimābātur* (W 205, M&F 51, ER 362, LFA 102, J 427, A&G 482 ff.).

   putārētur etiam cum nūminibus habēre sermōnem – *indirect discourse: personal construction with passive verbs of saying* (A&G 582). See note on *Trāditur . . . addūxisse*, line 13.

> The notion that Scipio was divinely inspired—part of the so-called Scipionic legend—arose during his lifetime (perhaps encouraged by him) and was later elaborated to include divine parentage.

119. **Secundō proeliō** – *ablative of time when* (no preposition is used) (W 99, M&F 116, ER 346, LFA 7, J 422, A&G 423). See note on *Nullō tamen Pūnicō bellō*, line 31.

   castra – neuter plural accusative (direct object). Translate as singular: *camp*.

   capit – The unstated subject is *Scīpiō*.

120. **XI mīlibus occīsīs** – *ablative absolute* (W 155, M&F 162, ER 348, LFA 33, J 29, A&G 419–20). **occīsīs** – perfect passive participle of *occīdō, -ere*.

121. **quī sē Āfrīs coniunxerat** – *coniunxerat* is pluperfect indicative to indi-

cate time prior to the historical present main verb, *capit*. **sē** – third person singular reflexive direct object. The gender and number of the third person reflexive pronoun are determined by the subject.

Numidiae rēgem – After Syphax was defeated in 203 BCE, Scipio recognized Masinissa as king of the Numidians. See Chapter XXII.

---

122. **nōbilissimīs** – superlative degree (W 172, M&F 150, ER 65, LFA 52, A&G 124) of the adjective *nōbilis*.

   Rōmam – *accusative of place to which:* no preposition is used with the names of cities (W 262, M&F 372, ER 345, LFA 204, J 418, A&G 427).

   ā Scīpiōne – *ablative of personal agent* (W 118, M&F 65, ER 346, LFA 33, J 420, A&G 405), with the passive verb *mittitur*.

123. **Quā rē audītā** – *ablative absolute* (W 155, M&F 162, ER 348, LFA 33, J 29, A&G 419). **audītā** – perfect passive participle of *audiō, -īre*. For **Quā** standing at the beginning of this sentence (M&F 115, LFA 204, A&G 308f), see note on *In quibus malīs*, line 34.

   omnis ferē Ītalia – The adverb is placed between the adjective and the noun, as often in Latin.

   ā Carthāginiēnsibus – *ablative of personal agent* (W 118, M&F 65, ER 346, LFA 33, J 420, A&G 405), with the passive verb *iubētur*.

124. **quam** – The antecedent is *Āfricam*.

Chapter XXI

125. **annō septimō decimō** – *ablative of time when* (no preposition is used) (W 99, M&F 116, ER 346, LFA 7, J 422, A&G 423).

   ab Hannibale – The *ablative of separation* sometimes takes *a* or *ab* (W 130, M&F 102, ER 348, LFA 214, J 419, A&G 400 ff.).

Hannibal departed Italy in June 203 BCE.

Carthāginiēnsium – What is the case? Compare to line 2.

127. **missī sunt** – perfect passive of *mittō, -ere*.

    Quadrāgintā et quinque diēbus – *Duration of time* is usually expressed by the accusative (with no preposition), but sometimes—as here—the ablative without a preposition is used (A&G 424b): *for forty-five days*.

    hīs indūtiae datae sunt – *indūtiae* is the subject of the passive verb *datae sunt; hīs* (referring to the Carthaginians) is the indirect object. Render the plural *indūtiae* into English as singular: *a truce.* **datae sunt** – perfect passive of *dō, dāre*.

    quōusque īre Rōmam et regredī possent – Some adverbs meaning *until* take the present or imperfect subjunctive in *temporal clauses* implying *intention* or *expectancy* (A&G 553): *until they would be able to go to Rome and return.* The use of *quōusque* in this construction is postclassical; classical usage would employ *dum* or *quoad*.

128. **regredī** – infinitive of deponent verb *regredior, -gredī: to return*.

    pondō – indeclinable substantive, *pounds;* used with numerals, as the usual measure of weight.

    ab hīs accepta sunt – Translate as *received from them* (i.e., the Carthaginians), rather than as an *ablative of personal agent—received by them* (i.e., the Romans)—because *hīs* at the beginning of this sentence refers to the Carthaginians. **accepta sunt** – perfect passive of *accipiō, -ere*.

129. **ex arbitriō** – *ablative of cause* (W 444, M&F 164, ER 346, LFA 499, J 42, A&G 404).

    pācem iussit . . . fierī – *infinitive with subject accusative* governed by *iubeō* (W 254, ER 365, LFA 508, J 78, A&G 563a).

130. **nē . . . redderent** – three *jussive noun clauses (indirect commands)* (W

253, M&F 52, ER 363, LFA 135, J 78, A&G 563) depending on the idea of commanding in *hīs condiciōnibus dedit: that they should not have . . . that they should give . . . and that they should return.*

Chapter XXII

133. **Hannibale veniente ad Āfricam** – *ablative absolute* (W 155, M&F 162, ER 348, LFA 33, J 29, A&G 419–20): literally, *with Hannibal coming into Africa*. What would be a better English translation? **veniente** – present active participle of *veniō, -īre*. The active form of the participle can also be used to form an ablative absolute (cf. *contrādīcente alterō consule*, line 28).

> **multa hostīlia** – The Carthaginians had seized a Roman convoy carrying provisions off the coast of Carthage. When a Roman delegation was sent to denounce what had happened, they were dismissed without answer and their ships were attacked upon departure.

134. **ab Āfrīs** – *ablative of personal agent with a passive verb* (W 118, M&F 65, ER 346, LFA 33, J 420, A&G 405).

   facta sunt – perfect passive of *faciō, -ere*.

   venientēs – present participle modifying *Lēgātī*.

   ā Rōmānīs – *ablative of personal agent with a passive verb* (W 118, M&F 65, ER 346, LFA 33, J 420, A&G 405).

135. **captī sunt** – perfect passive of *capiō, -ere*. Construe *sunt* with both *captī* and *dīmissī*.

   iubente Scīpiōne – *ablative absolute* (W 155, M&F 162, ER 348, LFA 33, J 29, A&G 419–20). **iubente** – present active participle of *iubeō, -ēre* (cf. *contrādīcente alterō consule*, line 28, and *Hannibale veniente ad Āfricam*, line 133).

   dīmissī – perfect passive participle of *dimittō, -ere*.

Hannibal . . . etiam ipse pācem – The English word order would be *Hannibal quoque (victus frequentibus proeliīs) ipse etiam petiit pācem ā Scīpiōne.*

frequentibus proeliīs – *ablative of time when* (no preposition is used) (W 99, M&F 116, ER 346, LFA 7, J 422, A&G 423). See note on *Nullō tamen Pūnicō bellō,* line 31.

136. **victus** – perfect passive participle of *vincō, -ere,* modifying *Hannibal.*

    petiit – contracted perfect form of *petīvit* (A&G 181). Some manuscripts have *petit,* which would be *historical present.*

> Hannibal was said to have sought a conference with Scipio prior to the battle of Zama to see if he could procure peace terms more favorable to the Carthaginians than had previously been offered.

Cum ventum esset ad colloquium – *cum clause (circumstantial)* (W 211, M&F 248, ER 361, LFA 504, J 213, A&G 546). **ventum esset** – perfect passive of *veniō, -īre.* The passive of intransitive verbs is often used impersonally (A&G 208d): *when it had come to a conference.* Translate as *when a conference had been held.* The pluperfect subjunctive is used here to denote action prior to that of the perfect main verb, *data est.* As usual, the subjunctive in the *cum clause* is rendered into English as indicative.

137. **īsdem condiciōnibus** – *ablative of manner* (W 92, M&F 50, ER 347, LFA 14, A&G 412). The preposition *cum* is not used when the ablative is modified by an adjective. **īsdem** – an alternate spelling of *eīsdem.* The suffix *-dem* does not decline; the first syllable indicates the case.

    data est – perfect passive of *dō, dāre.*

    additīs . . . propter novam perfidiam – *quingentīs mīlibus pondō argentī* is a *dative of indirect object* placed in the middle of the *ablative absolute, additīs centum mīlibus lībrārum.* The English word order would be *centum mīlibus lībrārum additīs quingentīs mīlibus pondō argentī propter* *novam perfidiam.* **additīs** – perfect passive participle of *addō, -ere.* **centum** – indeclinable numeral.

138. **lībrārum** – *partitive genitive* (W 98, M&F 154, ER 342, LFA 25, J 414, A&G 346).

139. **iussēruntque Hannibalem pugnāre** – *infinitive with subject accusative* governed by *iubeō* (W 254, ER 365, LFA 135, J 78, A&G 563a).

140. **Infertur . . . Carthāginī bellum** – The passive main verb, *infertur,* and the subject, *bellum,* are the first and last words of the sentence respectively. The syntax of the entire sentence is: *main verb,* followed by *two ablatives of personal agent* (with some additional information about the second person in the form of an *appositive* and a *relative clause*), followed by a dative indicating against whom the war was being waged, followed by the subject. *Infertur* is *historical present* (ER 23, LFA 501, A&G 469).

Masinissā – See note on *Numidiae rēgem,* page 57.

---

aliō rēge Numidārum – in apposition to *Masinissā* (W 19, M&F 363, LFA 8, A&G 282), and thus it is ablative in agreement.

quī – The antecedent is *Masinissā.*

142. **quōs captōs Scīpiō circumdūcī per castra iussit** – Translate as two coordinate clauses. See note on *Hasdrubalem . . . victum fugat,* line 90 (A&G 496 n. 2).

Scīpiō . . . iussit – governs four *infinitives with accusative subjects* (W 254, ER 365, LFA 135, J 78, A&G 563a): *quōs captōs circumdūcī, exercitum ostendī, prandium darī,* and *eōs dīmittī,* literally, *Scipio ordered them to be led about . . . the entire army to be shown . . . lunch to be given . . . and [them] to be dismissed.* What would be a more idiomatic English translation? See note on *eōs cīvēs nōn esse necessāriōs,* line 39.

143. **ut renuntiārent Hannibalī** – *purpose clause* (W 189, M&F 50, ER 362, LFA 77, J 68, A&G 529 ff.); *renuntiārent* is imperfect subjunctive and indicates an intended action *after* that of the historical main verb *iussit.*

144. **quae apud Rōmānōs vīdissent** – *indirect question* governed by *renun-tiārent* (W 204, M&F 202, ER 362, LFA 116, J 128, A&G 573 ff.); *vīdissent* is pluperfect subjunctive and indicates *time prior to renuntiārent*.

Chapter XXIII

145. **instructum est** – perfect passive of *instruō, -ere*.

146. **cum perītissimī . . . ēdūcerent** – *cum clause (causal)* (W 211, M&F 248, ER 361, LFA 504, J 213, A&G 549). Render *cum* in this clause as *since*. **perītissimī** – superlative degree of *perītus, -a, -um* (W 172, M&F 150, ER 65, LFA 52, A&G 124).

> That the contest between Scipio and Hannibal was between the two greatest generals of all time is a sentiment echoed by all the ancient historians.

147. **ipsō Hannibale captō, quī prīmum cum multīs equitibus . . . ēvāsit** – *ablative absolute* (W 155, M&F 162, ER 348, LFA 33, J 29, A&G 419–20) followed by a relative clause whose antecedent is *Hannibale*. **captō** – perfect passive participle of *capiō, -ere*. **ēvāsit** – perfect of *ēvādō, -ere*.

> The battle of Zama took place in the summer of 202 BCE. Hannibal's elephants were used at the opening of the battle with little effect, and Masinissa's decisive Numidian cavalry routed its Carthaginian counterpart. Since the infantries of the two armies were then more or less evenly matched, when the Roman cavalry attacked from the rear, Hannibal's army was completely defeated. See Appendix B: Maps and Battle Plans.

148. **Inventa** – perfect passive participle of *inveniō*, *-īre*. Supply *sunt*.

149. **argentī pondō vīgintī mīlia** – The English word order would be *vīgintī mīlia pondō argentī*. See note at line 128.

supellectilis – postclassical nominative singular form for *supellex*.

150. **facta est** – perfect passive of *faciō*, *-ere*.

151. **Rōmam** – accusative of place to which: no preposition is used with the names of cities (W 262, M&F 372, ER 345, LFA 204, J 418, A&G 427).

ingentī glōriā – ablative of manner (W 92, M&F 50, ER 347, LFA 14, A&G 412). See note on *ingentī glōriā*, line 78.

---

triumphāvit – A triumphal procession along the Via Sacra to the temple of Jupiter Capitolinus was celebrated by a successful Roman general upon his return from a campaign. The honor (until the late Republic) was granted only to a high-ranking magistrate who had been victorious over a foreign enemy. The procession consisted of the spoils of war (including captives), the victor on a horse-drawn chariot, the magistrates and Senate, and the victorious army.

Āfricānus – predicate nominative with a passive verb of naming (A&G 393a).

appellārī – passive infinitive.

152. **coeptus est** – perfect passive of *coepī*, *-isse*; the subject is *Scipiō*. *Coepī* is a defective verb that uses the perfect tenses only (*incipiō* is used for the present, imperfect, and future tenses) (A&G 205).

post . . . quam – *postquam* is regularly separated in expressions denoting definite intervals of time (days, months, years, etc.) and often takes the pluperfect, as here (A&G 543a).

H. H. SCULLARD ON THE CAUSES OF ROME'S SUCCESS

[T]he causes of [Hannibal's] failure were largely the causes of Rome's success: Rome's superiority at sea, her roads and fortresses, the unexpected loyalty of her Italian allies which morally justified her conquest of the Italian peninsula, the unshaken direction of the Senate, the loyal co-operation of the people and their "will to conquer," which survived disaster after disaster, the wisdom of a strategy of exhaustion and the courage by which it was maintained while the countryside bled, the blocking of reinforcements from Carthage and Spain, the undermining of the enemy's resources in the Spanish peninsula, and above all the superior quality of the vast manpower on which Rome could draw in her hour of need. Finally, what turned the hope of ultimate success against Hannibal into complete and devastating victory against Carthage was the production of a military genius by Rome, one who learning as a pupil from Hannibal himself forged out of the Roman army a weapon which could be turned against the master. Rome produced many generals of distinction but only one who dared face Hannibal in open battle after Cannae. Fabius was called the Shield of Rome and Marcellus her Sword, but Scipio's very name meant a Staff, on which Rome could lean and with which she could thrash her foe. But the brilliance of a Scipio would have been useless without that unswerving loyalty and perseverance of the Senate and the People of Rome. The unavailing gallantry of the great house of Barca at length succumbed to the solid moral qualities of the self-sacrifice of a nation at war. It was by moral forces that Rome survived her ordeal: forces which were soon to be blunted by ambition and avarice at home and by the contagious corruption of the eastern world into which she was next drawn.

A History of the Roman World 753–146 BC, pp. 238–39

Vocabulary

All inflected forms used in Book III of the *Breviarium* are listed in square brackets at the end of the entries.

The following abbreviations are used in this section:

abl.	ablative
acc.	accusative
adj.	adjective
adv.	adverb
comp.	comparative
conj.	conjunction
demonstr. pron.	demonstrative pronoun
f.	feminine
gen.	genitive
ind.	indicative
indecl.	indeclinable
indef. pron.	indefinite pronoun
m.	masculine
n.	neuter
num.	numeral
part.	participle
pass.	passive
pl.	plural
prep.	preposition
pron.	pronoun
reflex. pron.	reflexive pronoun
relat.	relative
rel. pron.	relative pronoun
sing.	singular
subj.	subjunctive
subst.	substantive
sup.	superlative

A

ā, ab (*ā* only before consonants, *ab* before vowels and some consonants), prep. with abl., 1. in space, *from, away from, out of;* 2. of time, *from, since, after;* 3. to denote the agent, *by;* 4. to denote source, origin, extraction, *from, of;* 5. with verbs of freeing from, defending, protecting, *from.*

abeō, -īre, -iī, -itum [ab + eō], *to go from, depart [abiēns].*

abstineō, -ēre, -tinuī, -tentum [abs + teneō], *restrain, refrain, abstain [abstinēret].*

accēdo, -ere, -cessī, -cessum [ad + cēdō], *to go or come to or near, to approach [accessit].*

accipiō, -ere, -cēpī, -ceptum [ad + capiō], *receive, get, accept, admit; deal with, treat* (line 32) *[accēperant, accēpit, accepta, acceptī, acciperet].*

ad, prep. with acc., 1. in space, *to, toward;* 2. in time, *about, toward;* 3. in number or amount, *near, near to, almost, about, toward.*

addō, -ere, -didī, -ditum [ad + dō], *to add to, lay on [additīs].*

addūcō, -ere, -dūxī, -ductum [ad + dūcō], *to lead to, bring to, bring along [addūxisse].*

adeō, adv., *to such a degree.*

adficiō, -ere, -fēcī, -fectum [ad + faciō], *to do something to one, to inflict upon, afflict [adficiuntur].*

adgredior, -ī, -gressus sum [ad + gradior], *to undertake, begin* (line 3); *to fall on, attack, assault* (line 79) *[adgressus].*

adhūc, adv., *until now, hitherto, as yet.*

admittō, -ere, -mīsī, -missum [ad + mittō], *let come, admit, give access [admittere].*

adventus, -ūs, m., *a coming, approach, arrival [adventū].*

adversus, prep with acc., *against, in opposition to [adversus].*

Aemilius, -ī, m., *Roman gens name.* **L. Aemilius Paulus**, *consul 216 BCE; defeated by Hannibal in battle of Cannae* (ch. X) *[Aemilius, Aemiliō].*

aetās, -ātis, f., *the life of man, age, lifetime, years [aetāte, aetātis].*

Āfrī, -ōrum, m. [pl. subst. from Āfer, Āfra, Āfrum], *the Carthaginians or their allies [Āfrī, Āfrōrum, Āfrīs].*

Āfrica, -ae, f., in a restricted sense, *the territory of Carthage [Āfricā, Āfricam].*

Āfricānus, -a, -um, adj., *pertaining to Africa, African; agnomen conferred upon P. Cornēlius Scīpiō after his victory over the Carthaginians [Āfricānus].*

agō, -ere, ēgī, actum, *act, do, perform, conduct; spend, live [agēns, ēgerat, ēgit].*

Agrigentum, -ī, n., *a Greek colony in southwestern Sicily (now Agrigento) [Agrigentum].*

aliter, adv. [alis], *in another manner, otherwise, in any other way, differently.*

alius, -a, -ud, adj., *another, other, different [aliīs, aliō].*

Alpes, -ium, f., *the high mountains of Switzerland, the Alps [Alpēs].*

alter, altera, alterum, adj., *another, the other [alterō, alterum].*

ambō, ambae, ambō, adj., *both (of a pair or couple) [ambō].*

amīcitia, -ae, f. [amicus], *friendship; league, alliance [amīcitiam].*

amīcus, -a, -um, adj. [amō], *friendly, amicable, favorable [amīcam].*

amnis, -is, m., *river [amnem].*

amplius, adv. [comp. of amplē], *more.*

animus, -ī, m., *mind, opinion* (line 89); *courage, spirit* (line 111) *[animus, animō].*

annus, -ī, m., *year [annum, annō, annōs].*

ante, adv., of time, *before, previously.*

ānulus, -ī, m., *ring,* esp. *for the finger [ānulōrum].*

Ap., *abbreviation of the praenomen Appius.*

apparātus, -ūs, m. [apparō], *apparatus, tools, implements, engines, supplies, material, instruments [apparātum].*

appellō, -āre, -āvī, -ātum, *to address; to call by name, to name [appellārī, appellātur].*

apud, prep. with acc., *at, near, by, with, among;* of physical proximity, *before, in the presence of.*

Āpūlia, -ae, f., *a region in southeastern Italy [Āpūliā, Āpūliam].*

arbitrium, -ī, n. [arbiter], *judgment, opinion, decision [arbitriō].*

argentum, -ī, n., *silver [argentī, argentum].*

Arīminum, -ī, n., *a town in Umbria in northern Italy on the Adriatic Sea (now Rimini) [Arīminum].*

armātus, -a, -um [part. of armō], *armed, equipped, in arms [armātī].*

Asia, -ae, f., *the continent of Asia; the peninsula of Asia Minor [Asiae].*

atque, in joining single words, *and,* and even; in connecting sentences and clauses, *and indeed, and so.*

Attalus, -ī, m., *Attalus I (241–219 BCE), king of Pergamum* (ch. XIV) *[Attalō].*

audiō, -īre, īvī or -iī, -ītum, *to hear, hear of, listen to [audītā].*

aureus, -a, -um, *of gold, golden [aureōrum].*

aurum, -ī, n., *gold [aurī, aurum].*

aut, conj., *or.*

auxilium, -ī, n., *help, aid, assistance, support [auxilia].*

B

bellum, -ī, n., *war, warfare [bellum, bellī, bellō].*

bene, adv. [bonus], *well.*

Brittiī, -ōrum, m., *the Bruttii, the inhabitants of the southern point of Italy, or their territory [Brittiī, Brittiōs].*

C

Caecilius, -ī, m., *Quintus Caecilius, consul 206 BCE [Caeciliō].*

caedō, -ere, cecīdī, caesum, *to cut, cut to pieces; kill, conquer, rout [caesa].*

Calabria, -ae, f., *a region in southern Italy [Calabriam].*

callidus, -a, -um, adj., *skillful, shrewd, crafty, cunning [callidum].*

Campānia, -ae, f., *a region in western Italy, south of Latium [Campāniae, Campāniam].*

Cannae, -ārum, f. pl., *a small town in Apulia, where one of the most important battles of the Second Punic War was fought, 216 BCE [Cannae].*

capiō, -ere, cēpī, captum, *to take, get,*

capiō, -ere, cēpī, captum (cont.)
seize, capture, arrive at [capī, capit,
capiuntur, capta, captae, captī, captō,
captōs, captum, captīque, captīs, cēpit].

captīvus, -a, -um, adj. [capiō], captive;
as subst., captīvus, -ī, m., captive,
prisoner of war [captīvīs, captīvōrum,
captīvōs].

captus, see capiō.

Carthāginiēnsis, -e, adj., Carthaginian;
as a subst., Carthāginiēnsēs, -ium,
the Carthaginians [Carthāginiēnsem,
Carthāginiēnsibus, Carthāginiēn-
sium].

Carthāgō, -inis, f., 1. Carthage, a city
founded by the Phoenicians on the
northern coast of Africa; 2. Carthāgō
Nova, a city founded by the Carthaginians on the eastern coast of Spain [Car-
thāginem, Carthāginī].

castrum, -ī, n., fortified place, town; pl.,
castra, -ōrum, camp [castra, castrīs].

cāsus, -ūs, m. [cadō], chance [cāsū].

centum, indecl. num., adj., hundred.

cēpī, see capiō.

certāmen, -inis, n. [certō], struggle, battle, engagement [certāmen].

(cēterus), -a, -um, adj. [m. nom. sing.
lacking], the rest (line 21); other (line
149) [cētera, cēterī].

circumdūcō, -ere, -dūxī, -ductum, to
lead around [circumdūcī].

cīvis, -is, m., citizen [cīvēs].

cīvitās, -ātis, f., state, community; city
[cīvitātem, cīvitātēs].

Claudius, -ī, m., Roman gens name. Appius Claudius Nerō, consul 207 BCE;
defeated Hasdrubal in the battle of
Metaurus (ch. XVIII); M. Claudius
Marcellus, consul 222 BCE; successfully defended Nola from attack by
Hannibal in 214 (ch. XII); took Syracuse in 211 (ch. XIV); killed in battle
by Hannibal in 208 (ch. XVI)
[Claudiō, Claudius].

Cn., abbreviation of the praenomen
Gnaeus.

coepī, -isse, coeptum, defective verb, to
begin [coeperant, coeperat, coepit, coep-
tus].

cognōscō, -ere, cognōvī, cognitum
[noscō], to learn, perceive, understand
[cognitā, cognitō].

colloquium, -ī, n. [con + loquor], conference [colloquium].

committō, -ere, -mīsī, -missum
[con + mittō], commit, bring about;
pugnam or proelium committere, to
begin battle [commissō].

condiciō, -ōnis, f. [condīcō], condition;
terms, stipulation [condiciōne, condiciōnēs, condiciōnibus].

condō, -ere, -didī, -ditum [con + dō], to
found [conditā].

conflīgō, -ere, -flīxī, -flictum
[con + flīgō], to fight, contend [con-
flīgit].

congregō, -āre, -āvī, -ātum [con + grex],
to collect, unite [congregātīs].

coniungō, -ere, -iunxī, -iunctum
[con + iungō], to join, to join together,
unite, ally [coniunxerat, coniunx-
ērunt].

conpōnō, -ere, -posuī, -positum
[con + pōnō], to place, lay, set [con-
positās].

consul, -ulis, m., consul, one of the two
chief magistrates of the Roman republic. They were elected annually, and
the year was generally called by their

names, e.g., M. Minuciō Rūfō P. Cornēliō cōnsulibus [consul, consule, consulem, consulēs, consulī, consulibus,
consulis, consulum]. See Appendix C:
Roman Magistracies.

consulāris, -e, adj. [cōnsul], *of a consul,
of consular rank;* as subst., *ex-consul*
[consulārēs].

contrā, prep. with acc., *against, opposite
to, contrary to.*

contrādīcō, -ere, -dīxī, -dictum [con-
trā + dīcō], *to contradict, oppose [con-
trādīcente].*

cōpia, -ae, f. [con + ops], *abundance,
supply;* pl., *troops, supplies; means,
force, wealth [cōpiae, cōpiās, cōpiīs].*

cōpiōsus, -a, -um, adj. [copia], *in abundance [cōpiōsa].*

Cornēlius, -ī, m., *a large and important
gens at Rome.* **L. Cornēlius Scīpiō,**
*younger brother of P. Cornelius Scipio
Africanus* (ch. XVI); **P. Cornēlius
Scīpiō (Asina),** *consul 221 BCE* (ch.
VII); **P. Cornēlius Scīpiō,** *father of P.
Cornelius Scipio Africanus; consul 218
BCE; wounded by Hannibal in the bat-
tle of Ticinus* (ch. IX); *carried out suc-
cessful campaigns in Spain* (chs. XI,
XIII); *slain by Hasdrubal* (ch. XIV); **P.
Cornelius Scīpiō Africānus,** *consul
205 BCE; great Roman general who de-
feated Hannibal at the battle of Zama*
(chs. XV–XXIII) [Cornēliī, Cornēlium,
Cornēlius].

cum, conj., of time, *when, while, when-
ever;* of cause, *since;* of concession,
although [cum].

cum, prep. with abl., *with, together with.*

D

datus, see *dō.*

dē, prep. with abl., *from, out of* (line 31);
concerning, in respect to (line 110).

dēceptus, see *dēcipiō.*

decimus, -a, -um [decem], num., adj.,
tenth [decimō, decimum].

dēcipiō, -ere, -cēpī, -ceptum [dē + capiō],
to catch, ensnare, entrap [dēceptī].

dēdī, see *dō.*

dēditiō, -ōnis, f. [dēdō], *surrender [dēdi-
tiōnem].*

dēdō, -ere, -didī, -ditum, f., *to give up,
surrender [dēdidērunt].*

deinde, adv. [dē + inde], *next, then.*

dēleō, -ēre, -ēvī, -ētum, *to destroy, over-
throw [dēlētīs].*

dēnuntiō, -āre, -āvī, -ātum [dē + nun-
tiō], *to announce, denounce, order,
threaten [dēnuntiāvērunt].*

dēserō, -ere, -uī, -tum [dē + serō], *to
leave, abandon, desert [dēserit, dē-
seruerat].*

dēspērō, -āre, -āvī, -ātum [dē + spērō],
to give up hope, despair [dēspērāns].

dētrahō, -ere, -trāxī, -tractum
[dē + trahō], *to strip off, remove [dē-
trāxerat].*

diēs, -ēī, m., *day [diēbus].*

differō, -ferre, distulī, dīlātum
[dis + ferō], *to delay, postpone [dif-
ferendō].*

diffīdō, -ere, -fīsus sum [dis + fidō], *to
distrust, doubt [diffīdere].*

diffugiō, -ere, -fūgī, — [dis + fugiō], *to
flee apart, scatter [diffūgērunt].*

dignor, -ārī, -ātus sum [dignus], *to
deem worthy, deign, condescend [dig-
nātus].*

dīmittō, -ere, -mīsī, -missum
[dis + mittō], *to send away, dismiss, release [dīmissī, dīmittīque].*

dispertiō, -īre, -īvī, -ītum [dis + partiō],
to distribute, divide [dispertīvit].

displiceō, -ēre, -uī, — [dis + placeō], *to displease [displicuērunt].*

diūtius, adv. [comp. of diū], *longer.*

dīvīnus, -a, -um, adj. [dīvus], *divine, sacred [dīvīnum].*

dō, dare, dedī, datum, *to give, put, place; furnish, yield [darent, darī, data, datae, dedit].*

duo, -ae, -o, num., adj., *two [duōbus].*

duodecim [duo + decem], indecl. num., adj., *twelve.*

dūrus, -a, -um, adj., *hard, harsh, difficult [dūra].*

dux, ducis, m. [ducō], *commander, general [duce, ducem, ducibus, dux].*

E

ēducō, -ere, -dūxī, -ductum [ex + dūcō],
to lead out [ēdūcerent].

ēgī, see *agō.*

ēgregius, -a, -um, adj. [ē + grex], *select, distinguished, eminent [ēgregiās].*

elephantus, -ī, m., *elephant [elephantī, elephantōs].*

enim, conj., always postpositive,
namely, in fact, you know, for, because.

eō, -īre, -iī, -itum, *to go, come, march [īre].*

eques, -itis, m. [equus], *horseman, knight;* pl., *cavalry [equitēs, equitibus, equitum].*

et, conj., *and, also, even, and yet;* **et . . . et**, *both . . . and.*

etiam, conj. [et + iam], *also, even.*

ēvādō, -ere, -vāsī, -vāsum [ex + vādō],
get away, escape [ēvāsit].

ēventus, -ūs, m. [ēveniō], *outcome, result [ēventū].*

ēvocō, -āre, -āvī, -ātum [ex + vocō], *to summon, call [ēvocāvērunt, ēvocāvit].*

ex, prep. with abl., 1. of place, *out of, from;* 2. of cause, *in consequence of, because of; according to.*

exercitus, -ūs, m. [exerceō], *army [exercitū, exercitum, exercitus].*

existimō, -āre, -āvī, -ātum
[ex + aestimō], *to judge, think, believe, suppose, imagine [existimābātur].*

explōrātor, -ōris, m. [explōrō], *scout [explōrātōrēs].*

expugnō, -āre, -āvī, -ātum [ex + pugnō],
to capture, overpower [expugnāvit].

F

Fabius, -ī, m., *Roman gens name.* Q.
Fabius Maximus Cunctātor, *the Roman opponent of Hannibal in the Second Punic War; named "Cunctator" from his policy of avoiding a general engagement with Hannibal's army* (chs. IX, X, XVI) *[Fabiō, Fabiōque, Fabius].*

faciō, -ere, fēcī, factum, *to do, make, act, form; choose, appoint;* present passive system supplied by **fīō, fierī**, *to be done, be made, occur, take place, happen [facta, factī, factus, fēcerat, fēcit, fierī].*

famēs, -is, f., *hunger, starvation [fame].*

fēcī, see *faciō.*

ferē, adv., *almost, nearly, for the most part, usually.*

fierī, see *faciō.*

fīlius, -ī, m., *son [fīlius].*

finis, -is, m., *end [finem].*

fiscus, -ī, m., *state treasury [fiscum].*

Flāminius, -ī, m., *Roman gens name.*
C. Flāminius Nepōs, *consul 223 BCE, defeated by Hannibal at Lake Trasimene* (ch. IX) *[Flāminiō, Flāminium].*

frangō, -ere, frēgī, fractum, *to break; wreck, subdue, tire out [fractā, frēgit].*

frāter, -tris, m., *brother [frāter, frātre, frātrem].*

frēgī, see frangō.

frequens, -entis, adj., *repeated, frequent [frequentibus].*

frūmentum, -ī, n. [fruor], *grain, corn;* pl., *crops [frūmenta].*

fugō, -āre, -āvī, -ātum [fugiō], *to put to flight, rout [fugat, fugātīs].*

Fulvius, -ī, m., *Roman gens name.* **Gn. Fulvius (Centumalus Maximus),** *consul 211 BCE [Fulviō, Fulvium].*

G

Gallī, -ōrum, m. [pl. subst. from Gallus, -a, -um], *the Gauls [Gallī].*

gerō, -ere, gessī, gestum, *perform, do, carry out* (line 102); *wage* (lines 7, 83) *[gereret, gerit, gesserat].*

glōria, -ae, f., *glory, honor, fame [glōriā].*

Gracchus, -ī, m., *Roman family name.* **Ti. Sempronius Gracchus,** *consul 218 BCE; defeated by Hannibal at the battle of Trebia* (ch. IX) *[Gracchus].*

Graecī, -ōrum, m. [pl. subst. from Graecus, -a, -um], *the Greeks [Graecōs].*

Graecia, -ae, f., *Greece [Graeciae].*

gravius, comp. adv. [gravis, -e], *more harshly, more severely.*

H

habeō, -ēre, -uī, -itum, *to have, hold, possess, keep; regard, consider [habēbant, habēre, habērent].*

Hannibal, -alis, m., *the great Carthaginian general of the Second Punic War, son of Hamilcar Barca [Hannibal, Hannibale, Hannibalem, Hannibalī, Hannibalis].*

Hannō, -ōnis, m., 1. *a Carthaginian general in the Second Punic War, taken captive in Sicily, 210 BCE* (ch. XIV); 2. *a Carthaginian general in the Second Punic war, defeated by Scipio, 203 BCE* (ch. XX) *[Hannōnem].*

Hasdrubal, -alis, m., 1. (the Bald) *commander of the Carthaginian expedition to Sardinia in the Second Punic War, 215 BCE* (ch. XIII, *alterum Hasdrubalem*); 2. (Barca) *brother of Hannibal, defeated and slain at the battle of the Metaurus, 207 BCE* (chs. VIII, XI, XIII, XIV, XV, XVIII) *[Hasdrubal, Hasdrubale, Hasdrubalem].*

hic, haec, hoc, demonstr. pron., *this; he, she, it; the following; the latter [hāc, haec, hīs, huic, hunc].*

Hispānī, -ōrum, m. [pl. subst. from Hispānus, -a -um], *the Spaniards [Hispānīs, Hispānōrum].*

Hispānia, -ae, f., *Spain (including Portugal) [Hispāniā, Hispāniae, Hispāniam, Hispāniārum, Hispāniās]*

homō, hominis, m. and f., *human being; man, mankind [hominum].*

hostīlis, -e, adj. [hostis], *hostile [hostīlia].*

I

iam, adv., *now, already, at once.*

ibi, adv., *there.*

ibīdem, adv. [ibi], *in that very place, in the same place.*

idem, eadem, idem, demonstr. pron., *the same [eōdem, īsdem].*

igitur, adv., *then, therefore, accordingly.*

ille, illa, illud, demonstr. pron., *that; he, she, it; the former [ille].*

impatiēns, -entis, adj. [in + patiēns], *impetuous [inpatientem].*

impatientia, -ae, f. [inpatiens], *impatience [inpatientiā].*

impetus, -ūs, m. [in + petō], *force, violence [impetū].*

in, prep. with acc., 1. of place, *into, to, on, upon, towards, against;* 2. of purpose, *for, with a view to;* 3. with abl., of place, *in, on, upon, in the midst of, among;* 4. of time, *in, in the course of, during.*

incidō, -ere, -cidī, — [in + cadō], *to fall, fall in with, meet [incidit].*

inclitus, -a, -um, adj., *famous, celebrated, glorious [inclitās].*

inde, adv., *from that place, thence.*

indīcō, -ere, -dīxī, -dictum [in + dīcō], *to proclaim, declare [indictum].*

indūtiae, -ārum, f. pl., *truce, armistice [indūtiae].*

inesse, see *insum*.

inferō, -ferre, intulī, inlātum [in + ferō], *to bring in or upon;* **bellum inferre**, *to wage war [infertur, inlātum].*

infinītus, -a, -um, adj. [in + finiō], *unbounded, vast, enormous [infīnītīs].*

ingēns, -entis, adj., *large, huge, great [ingēns, ingentēs, ingentī].*

inlātus, see *inferō*.

insequor, -ī, -secūtus sum [in + sequor], *to follow, follow after, come next [insequentī].*

insidiae, -ārum [insideō], f. pl., *ambush [insidiās].*

instruō, -ere, -strūxī, -structum [in + struō], *to prepare, make ready [instructum].*

insum, inesse, infuī, — [in + sum], *to be in [inesse].*

integer, -gra, -grum, adj. [in + tangō], *untouched, entire [integer].*

intereā, adv. [inter + is], *in the meantime, meanwhile.*

interficiō, -ere, -fēcī, -fectum [inter + faciō], *to slay, kill [interfēcit, interfectae, interficit, interficiuntur].*

interim, adv., *meanwhile.*

interimō, -ere, -ēmī, -emptum [inter + emō], *to kill [interēmit].*

invādō, -ere, -vāsī, -vāsum, *attack, seize [invādit].*

inveniō, -īre, -vēnī, -ventum [in + veniō], *to find, discover [inventa, inventā].*

invius, -a, -um, adj. [in + via], *without roads, impassible [inviās].*

ipse, -a, -um, intensive pron., *himself, herself, itself, themselves [ipse, ipsī, ipsō, ipsum].*

īre, see *eō*.

is, ea, id, demonstr. pron., *this, that; he, she, it; such [ea, eā, eam, eī, ēius, eō, eōrum, eōs, eum, eumque, id, is].*

īsdem, see *idem*.

ita, adv. [is], *in this way, so, thus; as follows, in such a way; accordingly, and so.*

Ītalia, -ae, f., *Italy [Ītalia, Ītaliā, Ītaliae, Ītaliam].*

itaque, adv. [ita + que], *and so, therefore, consequently.*

iter, itineris, n. [eō], *road, way, highway [itinere].*

iubeō, -ēre, iussī, iussum, *to order, command [iubente, iubētur, iussērunt, iussēruntque, iussit].*

K

Karthalō, -ōnis, m., *a Carthaginian general, slain by Q. Fabius Maximus* (ch. XVI) *[Karthalōnem].*

L

L., *abbreviation of the praenomen Lucius.*

laetitia, -ae, f. [laetus], *joy, rejoicing [laetitia].*

Laevīnus, -ī, m., *Roman family name.* **L. Valerius (Laevīnus)**, *consul 206 BCE* (ch. XIX); **M. Valerius Laevīnus**, *consul 210 BCE* (chs. XII, XIII, XIV) *[Laevīnō, Laevīnum, Laevīnus].*

lēgātus, -ī, m. [legō], *ambassador, legate; lieutenant, deputy [lēgātī, lēgātīs, lēgātōs].*

līberō, -āre, -āvī, -ātum [līber], *to set free, release [līberāta].*

lībra, -ae, f., *as a weight, a Roman pound [lībrārum].*

Ligurēs, -um, m. pl., *the people of Liguria, a region on the northwestern coast of Italy [Ligurēs].*

Līvius, -ī, m., *Roman gens name.* **M. Līvius Salīnātōr**, *consul 210 BCE; defeated Hasdrubal in the battle of Metaurus* (ch. XVIII) *[Līviō].*

locus, -ī, m., *place [locīs].*

M

M., *abbreviation of the praenomen Marcus.*

Macedonia, -ae, f., *a kingdom north of Greece in the southeastern Balkans, between Thessaly and Thrace [Macedoniā, Macedoniae, Macedoniam].*

magis, adv. [comp. of magnopere], *more, rather.*

magnus, -a, -um, adj., comp. **maior**, sup. **maximus**, *great, large, abundant, powerful [magna, magnō, magnum, maximam].*

Māgō, -ōnis, m., *Hannibal's brother, captured by Scipio in Spain* (chs. XIII, XV) *[Māgō, Māgōnem].*

male, adv. [malus], *badly, ill, unhappily, unsuccessfully.*

malus, -a, -um, adj., *bad, evil, hurtful;* as subst., **malum, -ī**, n., *misfortune [malīs].*

mandō, -āre, -āvī, -ātum [manus + dō], *command, send word [mandārētur].*

maneō, -ēre, mansī, mansum, *to stay, remain, continue [mansit].*

Manlius, -ī, m., *Roman gens name.* **T. Manlius Torquātus**, *consul 235 BCE; defeated Carthaginian forces in Sardinia in 215* (ch. XII) *[Manliō, Manlium, Manlius].*

manūmittō, -ere, -mīsī, -missum [manus + mittō], *to set free, emancipate [manūmissī].*

manus, -ūs, f., *hand, arm; band, troop; force; combat [manibus].*

Marcellus, -ī, m., *Roman family name.* **M. Claudius Marcellus**, *consul 222 BCE; successfully defended Nola from attack by Hannibal in 214* (ch. XII);

M. Claudius Marcellus (*cont.*)
took *Syracuse in 211* (ch. XIV); *killed
in battle by Hannibal in 208* (ch. XVI)
[*Marcellō, Marcellus*].

Masinissa, -ae, m., *king of Numidia, an
ally of the Romans* (ch. XXII) [*Masinissā*].

maximus, sup. of *magnus*.

Maximus, -ī, m., *Roman family name*.
Q. Fabius Maximus Cunctator, *the
Roman opponent of Hannibal in the
Second Punic War; named "Cuncta-
tor" from his policy of avoiding a gen-
eral engagement with Hannibal's army*
[*Maximō, Maximus*].

memoria, -ae, f. [memor], *memory* [*memoriā*].

mentiō, -ōnis, f., *mention* [*mentiōnem*].

metus, -ūs, m., *fear, dread* [*metū*].

mīles, -itis, m. and f., *soldier* [*mīlitēs,
mīlitibus, mīlitum*].

mīliārium, -ī, n., *milestone, mile* [*mīliārium*].

mille, indecl. num., adj., *thousand;*
mīlia, -ium, n. pl., *thousand, thou-
sands* [*mīlia, mīlibus, mīlium, mille*].

Minucius, -ī, m., *Roman gens name*. **M.
Minucius Rūfus,** *consul 221 BCE* (ch.
VII) [*Minuciō*].

mittō, -ere, mīsī, missum, *to send, dis-
patch* [*mīsērunt, mīsit, missī, missus,
mittit, mittitur*].

modius, -ī, m. [modus], *a Roman dry
measure approximately equal to one
peck (8 quarts or 537.6 cubic inches)*
[*modiōs*].

moneō, -ēre, -uī, -itum, *to advise, warn,
remind* [*monuit*].

mox, adv., *soon, directly, then*.

multus, -a, -um, adj., *much, many;* pl.,
many [*multa, multae, multās, multī,
multīs, multōs*].

N

nam, conj., *for, but*.

nascor, -ī, nātus sum, *to be born; spring
from, arise* [*nātus*].

nāvis, -is, f., *ship, vessel* [*nāvēs*].

nē, 1. adv., *not;* 2. conj., *in order that
not, lest, not to*.

necessārius, -a, -um, adj. [necesse],
necessary, indispensable [*necessāriōs*].

nēmō, -inis, m. and f. [nē + homō], *no
one* [*nēmō*].

Nerō, -ōnis, m., *Roman family name*.
Appius Claudius Nerō, *consul 207
BCE; defeated Hasdrubal in the battle
of Metaurus* (ch. XVIII) [*Nerōne*].

nōbilis, -e, adj. [noscō], *noted, notable;
renowned; noble, of noble birth* [*nōbilēs, nōbilibus, nōbilissima, nōbilissimīs, nōbilissimōs*].

Nōla, -ae, f., *a city in Campania in Italy*
[*Nōlam*].

nōlō, nōlle, nōluī, — [nē + volō], *to be
unwilling, not to wish, not to want*
[*nōluit*].

nōn, adv., *not, no*.

nōnus, -a, -um [novem], num., adj.,
ninth [*nōnum*].

novus, -a, -um, adj., *new, recent*
[*novam*].

nullus, -a, -um, adj. [ne + ullus], *none,
no* [*nullō, nullus*].

nūmen, -inis, n. [nuō], *divinity, deity,
god, goddess* [*nūminibus*].

Numidae, -ārum, m. pl., *the Numidians*
[*Numidārum, Numidīs*].

Numidia, -ae, f., *a kingdom of northern Africa, west of Carthage [Numidiae].*

numquam, adv. [ne + umquam], *never.*

nuntius, -ī, m., *message [nuntium].*

O

obpugnō, -āre, -āvī, -ātum [ob + pugnō], *to fight against, assault, besiege [obpugnāre].*

obses, -idis, m. and f. [obsideō], *hostage [obsidēs].*

obtulī, see *offerō.*

occāsiō, -ōnis, f. [occīdō, to happen], *occasion, opportunity [occāsiōne].*

occīdō, -ere, -cīdī, -cīsum [ob + caedō], *to cut down, kill, slay [occīdit, occīduntur, occīsa, occīsī, occīsīs, occīsus].*

occupō, -āre, -āvī, -ātum [ob + capiō], *to take possession of, seize, occupy [occupāvit].*

occurrō, -ere, -currī, -cursum [ob + currō], *to run to meet; meet with, encounter [occurrit].*

octō, indecl. num., adj., *eight.*

octōgintā [octō], indecl. num., adj., *eighty.*

offerō, -ferre, obtulī, oblātum, *to bring before, offer [obtulit].*

omnis, -e, adj., *every, all [omne, omnēs, omnī, omnibus, omnis, omnium].*

oppidum, -ī, n., *walled town [oppidō].*

ostendō, -ere, -ī, -tentum, *to show, exhibit, display [ostendīque].*

P

P., *abbreviation of the praenomen Publius.*

paene, adv., *almost, nearly.*

parēns, -entis, m. and f. [pariō], *father or mother, parent [parentibus].*

pāreō, -ēre, -uī, —, *to obey, serve, be subject to [pāruerant].*

pars, partis, f., *part, number; district; side, direction; party, faction [pars, parte].*

patefaciō, -ere, -fēcī, -factum [pateō + faciō], *to lay open [patefēcit].*

Paulus, -ī, m., *Roman family name (often spelled Paullus). L. Aemilius Paulus, consul 216 BCE; defeated by Hannibal in the battle of Cannae (ch. X) [Paulō, Paulus].*

pāx, pācis, f., *peace [pācem, pācis, pāx].*

pecūnia, -ae, f. [pecus], *money [pecūniam].*

pedes, -itis, m. [pēs], *foot soldier, infantry [peditum].*

per, prep. with acc., 1. *of place, through, across, over, throughout;* 2. *of time, through, during;* 3. *of means or agency, by means of, by the agency of, through.*

perdō, -ere, -didī, -ditum [per + dō], *to lose [perdit].*

pereō, -īre, -iī, -itum [per + eō], *to perish, disappear, die [pereunt, periit].*

perferō, -ferre, -tulī, -lātum [per + ferō], *to carry through [perlāta].*

perfidia, -ae, f. [perfidus], *treachery [perfidiam].*

perfuga, -ae, m. [perfugiō, to flee for refuge], *fugitive, deserter [perfugās].*

periī, see *pereō.*

perītus, -a, -um, adj., *skillful, experienced, familiar with [perītissimī].*

perlātus, see *perferō.*

petō, -ere, -īvī (iī), -ītum, *to strive for, seek; beg, ask, request [petiit, petīvērunt].*

Philippus, -ī, m., *Philip V, king of Mac-*

Philippus, -ī (*cont.*)
edonia, 220–178 BCE (ch. XII–XIV)
*[Philippī, Philippō, Philippum, Phi-
lippus].*

Pīcēnum, -ī, n., *a region of Italy on the
Adriatic Sea, north of Latium [Pīcēnī].*

poena, -ae, f., *punishment, penalty
[poenīs].*

pondō, adv. [old abl. from pondus], *by
weight;* with numerals, as an indecl.
subst., *pounds.*

pondus, -eris, n. [pendō], *weight
[pondus].*

poposcī, see *poscō.*

populus, -ī, m., *people, nation [populī,
populīs].*

porta, -ae, f., *city gate, gate [portam].*

poscō, -ere, poposcī, —, *to ask, demand
[poposcit].*

possum, posse, potuī, — [potis + sum],
*to be able, can [posse, possent, potuis-
sent].*

post, 1. adv., *after, later, afterwards;* 2.
prep. with acc., *after, behind.*

posteā, adv. [post + is], *afterwards;* with
quam, *after that, after which [posteā,
posteāquam].*

posterior, -us, gen. **-ōris**, adj. [comp. of
posterus, -a, -um], *later [posteriōre].*

postquam or **post . . . quam**, conj.
[post + quam], *after, when [postquam,
post . . . quam].*

postrēmō, adv. [posterus], *at last, finally.*

postulātiō, -ōnis, f., *demand, request;
complaint, application for redress [pos-
tulātiōnēs, Commentary only].*

potuī, see *possum.*

praeda, -ae, f., *booty, spoil, plunder
[praeda, praedam].*

praetor, -ōris, m. [prae + eō], *praetor,
magistrate [praetōriī].* See Appendix
C: Roman Magistracies.

prandium, -ī, n., *lunch [prandium].*

prīmum, adv. [prīmus], *first.*

prīmus [sup. of prior], *first, foremost
[prīmus].*

prius, adv. [prior], *before, sooner, previously.*

prōconsul, -is, m. [prō + consul], *proconsul, governor of a province (esp. after having served as consul)
[prōconsule, prōconsulem].* See Appendix C: Roman Magistracies.

proelium, -ī, n., *battle, combat, engagement [proeliīs, proeliō, proelium].*

proficiscor, -ī, -fectus sum [pro + fa-
ciscor], *to set out, proceed [profectus].*

prōmittō, -ere, -mīsī, -missum
[pro + mittō], *promise, assure [prōmit-
tēns].*

propter, prep. with acc., *on account of.*

pugna, -ae, f., *combat, fight, battle
[pugnā, pugnam].*

pugnō, -āre, -āvī, -ātum [pugna], *to
fight; oppose, resist [pugnābātur, pugnāns, pugnāre, pugnat, pugnātum,
pugnāvit].*

Pūnicus, -a, -um, adj., *Phoenician,
Punic; Carthaginian [Pūnicō,
Pūnicum].*

putō, -āre, -āvī, -ātum, *to think, consider,
suppose [putārētur].*

Pȳrēnaeus, -a, -um, adj. as a subst., *the
Pyrenees mountains [Pȳrēnaeum].*

Q

Q., *abbreviation of the praenomen
Quintus.*

quadrāgēsimus, -a, -um [quadrāgintā], num., adj., *fortieth [quadrāgēsimō]*.

quadrāgintā or XL, num., adj., *forty [quadrāgintā]*.

quālis, -e, adj., relat., *of such a kind, such as, the likes of which, as [quāle]*.

quārē, adv. [quā + rē], relat., *for which reason, wherefore, therefore*.

quartus, -a, -um [quattuor], num., adj., *fourth [quartō, quartum]*.

quattuor, indecl. num., adj., *four*.

quī, quae, quod, 1. rel. pron., *who, which, what, that;* 2. in place of a conj. and demonstr. pron., *and this, and that* (lines 34, 51, 71, 90, 117, 123) *[cuī, quā, quae, quam, quem, quī, quibus, quō, quod, quōs]*.

quīdam, quaedam, quiddam (pron.) or quoddam (adj.), indef. pron. and adj.; as a pron., *a certain one, someone, something* (line 117); as an adj., *a certain* (line 75) *[quendam, quiddam]*.

quingentēsimus, -a, -um [quīngenti], num., adj., *five hundredth [quingentēsimō]*.

quingentī, -ae, [quīnque + centum], num., adj., *five hundred [quingenta, quingentī, quingentīs]*.

quinque, indecl. num., adj., *five*.

quoque, adv., *also, too*.

quōusque, adv., *until what time*.

R

recēdō, -ere, -cessī, -cessum, *to go away, depart [recēdit]*.

recipiō, -ere, -cēpī, -ceptum [re + capiō], *to receive, take back, retake, recover; admit;* sē recipere, *to retreat [recēpērunt, recēpit, receptā]*.

redeō, -īre, -iī, -itum, *to go back, return [redderent, reddidit, rediit, redīre]*.

redimō, -ere, -ēmī, -emptum [re + emō], *to buy back, redeem, ransom [redimerent]*.

referō, -ferre, -tulī, -lātum [re + ferō], *to bring back [relātum, retulit]*.

regredior, -gredī, -gressus sum [re + gradior], *to step back, retreat, return [regredī, regressus]*.

relātus, see *referō*.

relinquō, -ere, -līquī, -lictum [re + linquō], *to leave behind, leave [relictō]*.

remaneō, -ēre, -mansī, — [re + maneō], *to remain behind [remanserat]*.

rēnuntiō, -āre, -āvī, -ātum [re + nuntiō], *to carry back word, report [renuntiārent]*.

reparō, -āre, -āvī, -atum [re + parō], *to renew, restore [reparandās]*.

reportō, -āre, -āvī, -ātum [re + portō], *to carry back, report [reportāvit]*.

rēs, reī, f., *thing, matter; affair, deed, exploit, event; circumstance, trouble [rē, rēs]*.

respondeō, -ēre, -spondī, -sponsum [re + spondeō], *to answer, reply, respond [responsumque]*.

responsum, -ī, n. [respondeō], *answer [responsa]*.

retineō, -ēre, -tinuī, -tentum [re + teneō], *to hold, retain [retinērī]*.

retulī, see *referō*.

rex, rēgis, m. [regō], *king [rēge, rēgem, rex]*.

Rōma, -ae, f., Rome *[Rōmae, Rōmam]*.

Rōmānus, -a, -um, adj., *Roman;* as subst., Rōmānī, -ōrum, m. pl., *the Romans [Rōmānī, Rōmānīs, Rōmānōrum, Rōmānōs, Rōmānus]*.

Rūfus, -ī, m., *Roman family name.* M.

Rūfus, -ī (*cont.*)
Minucius Rūfus, *consul 221 BCE* (ch. VII) *[Rūfō]*.
rursus, adv., *back; again.*

S

Saguntīnī, -ōrum, m. pl., *the inhabitants of Saguntum [Saguntīnī].*
Saguntum, -ī, n., *a city on the eastern coast of Spain [Saguntum].*
Salīnātōr, -ōris, m., **M. Līvius Salīnātōr**, *consul 210 BCE; defeated Hasdrubal in the battle of Metaurus* (ch. XVIII) *[Salīnātōre].*
Sardī, -ōrum, m. pl., *the Sardinians, inhabitants of the island of Sardinia [Sardōs].*
Sardinia, -ae, f., *Sardinia, an island in the Mediterranean Sea, west of Italy [Sardinia, Sardiniā, Sardiniam].*
sauciō, -āre, -āvī, -ātum [saucius], *to wound [sauciātur].*
Scīpiō, -ōnis, m., *the name of one of the most illustrious families of Rome; L.* **Cornēlius Scīpiō**, *younger brother of P. Cornelius Scipio Africanus* (ch. XVI); **P. Cornēlius Scīpiō (Asina)**, *consul 221 BCE* (ch. VII); **P. Cornēlius Scīpiō**, *father of P. Cornelius Scipio Africanus; consul 218 BCE; wounded by Hannibal in the battle of Ticinus* (ch. IX); *carried out successful campaigns in Spain* (chs. XI, XIII); *slain by Hasdrubal* (ch. XIV); **P. Cornēlius Scīpiō Africānus**, *consul 205 BCE; great Roman general who defeated Hannibal at the battle of Zama* (chs. XV–XXIII) *[Scīpiō, Scīpiōne, Scīpiōnem, Scīpiōnēs, Scīpiōnibus, Scīpiōnis].*

secundus, -a, -um, adj. [sequor], *second [secundō, secundum].*
sed, conj., *but, yet.*
Semprōnius, -ī, m., **Ti. Semprōnius Gracchus**, *consul 218 BCE; defeated by Hannibal at the battle of Trebia* (ch. IX) *[Semprōnius].*
Sēna, -ae, f., *a port city in Umbria in Italy, usually called Sēna Gallica [Sēnam].*
senātor, -ōris, m. [senātus], *senator [senātōrēs, senātōrum].*
senātus, -ūs, m., *the senate, chief power in the Roman state [senātū, senātum, senātus].*
septem, indecl. num., adj., *seven.*
septimus, -a, -um [septem], num., adj., *seventh [septimō].*
sermō, -ōnis, m., *talk, conversation, discourse [sermōnem].*
servus, -ī, m., *slave, servant [servī].*
Sicilia, -ae, f., *the island of Sicily [Siciliā, Siciliae, Siciliam].*
socius, -ī, m., *ally, confederate [sociōs].*
sollicitō, -āre, -āvī, -ātum [sollicitus, agitated], *to incite, stir, agitate [sollicitāta].*
spolium, -ī, n., *spoil, booty [spoliīs].*
strēnuē, adv. [strenuus], *vigorously.*
sub, prep. with acc., *under, towards, until, after;* with abl., *under, beneath, close to.*
subigō, -ere, -ēgī, -actum [sub + agō], *to conquer, subjugate, subdue [subacta, subigeret].*
subitō, adv. [subitus], *suddenly.*
succēdō, -ere, -cessī, -cessum [sub + cēdō], *to succeed, follow, take the place of [succēdunt].*
suī (gen.), **sibi** (dat.), **sē** (acc. and abl.), reflex. pron., sing. and pl., *himself, herself, itself, themselves [sē, sibi].*

Sulpicius, -ī, m., P. Sulpicius (Galba), *consul 211 BCE [Sulpiciō].*

sum, esse, fuī, futūrum, *to be, exist, live;* with gen., *belonging to, be a part of; be true, be so; happen, take place;* with dat., *have, possess [erant, erat, esse, essent, esset, est, fuerant, fuerat, fuit, sunt].*

supellectilis, -lectilis, f. [classical nominative, supellex], *equipment [supellectilis].*

supplicium, -ī, n., *torture, mode of execution [suppliciīs].*

suus, -a, -um [suī], pron., adj., *his own, her own, its own, their own; his, her, its, their;* as subst., **suī, -ōrum,** m. pl., *his (their) friends, men, troops, forces [suā, suās, suīs, suum].*

Syphāx, -ācis, m., *a king of Numidia* (ch. XX) *[Syphācem, Syphāx].*

Syrācūsānus, -a, -um, adj., *belonging to Syracuse;* **urbs Syrācūsāna,** *the city of Syracuse [Syrācūsāna].*

T

T., *abbreviation of the praenomen Titus.*

tamen, adv., *notwithstanding, yet, still, for all that, all the same, however, nevertheless.*

Tarentum, -ī, n., *a flourishing Greek city on the southern coast of Italy [Tarentum].*

tempus, -oris, n., *time, period, season [tempore].*

teneō, -ēre, -uī, tentum, *to hold, keep, possess; maintain, guard, defend; seize [tenēbantur, tenēre].*

Terentius, -ī, m., **(C.) Terentius Varrō,** *consul 216 BCE, defeated by Hannibal in the battle of Cannae* (ch. X) *[Terentius].*

tertius, -a, -um [trēs], num., adj., *third [tertiō, tertius].*

Ti., *abbreviation of the praenomen Tiberius.*

Torquātus, -ī, m., **T. Manlius Torquātus,** *consul 235 BCE; defeated Carthaginian forces in Sardinia in 215 [Torquātum].*

tōtus, -a, -um, adj., *all, all the, the whole, entire [tōtam, tōtum].*

trādō, -ere, -didī, -ditum [trans + dō], *to give over, give up, deliver;* **trāditur,** *he is said [trādidērunt, trāditur].*

trāiciō, -ere, -iēcī, -iectum [trans + iaciō], *carry across, transport [traiēcit].*

transeō, -īre, -iī, -itum [trans + eō], *to go over, to go across, cross, to cross over [transierant, transiērunt, transiit].*

transferō, -ferre, -tulī, -lātum [trans + ferō], *transfer, turn, change [transtulērunt].*

Trebia, -ae, f., *a river in Cisalpine Gaul, where the second battle of the Second Punic War was fought [Trebiam].*

trēs, trīa, num., adj., *three [trēs, trīa].*

trīgintā, indecl. num., adj., *thirty.*

triumphō, -āre, -āvī, -ātum, *to celebrate a triumph [triumphāvit].*

tum, adv., *then, at that time; thereupon.*

turbō, -āre, -āvī, -ātum [turba], *to disturb, confuse [turbāta].*

Tuscia, -ae, f., *Etruria, a region of central Italy [Tusciam].*

U

ubi, adv., *where, when.*

ullus, -a, -um, *any [ullā].*

ultimus, -a, -um, adj. [sup. of ulterior],
  farthest, last, utmost, greatest [ultimīs].
ūnus, -a, -um, adj., *one, only, sole, alone*
  [ūnō].
urbs, urbis, f., *city; The City (Rome)*
  [urbe, urbis, urbs].
usque, adv., *all the way, right on, contin-*
  uously, even.
ut, conj., 1. with ind., *when;* 2. with
  subj. of purpose, *in order that, that;*
  3. with subj. of result, *so that, that.*
uterque, utraque, utrumque, adj.
  [uter + que], *each (of two), both [utrō-*
  que].

V

Valerius, -ī, m., *Roman gens name.* **L.
  Valerius (Laevīnus)**, *consul 206 BCE*
  (ch. XIX); **M. Valerius Laevīnus**, *consul 210 BCE* (chs. XII, XIII, XIV)
  [Valeriō, Valerium].
varius, -a, -um, adj., *diverse, various*
  [variīs].
Varrō, -ōnis, m., **(C.) Terentius Varrō**,
  *consul 216 BCE, defeated by Hannibal
  in the battle of Cannae* (ch. X) *[Varrō,
  Varrōnis].*
vastō, -āre, -āvī, -ātum, *to lay waste, dev-
  astate, destroy [vastābat].*

vendō, -ere, -didī, -ditum, *to sell [ven-
  didit, venditōrum].*
veniō, -īre, vēnī, ventum, *to come, go,
  approach [vēnerat, veniente, venientēs,
  venientium, vēnit, ventum].*
vērum, adv. [vērus], *but.*
vīcēsimus, -a, -um [vīgintī], num., adj.,
  twentieth [vīcēsimum].
vīcī, see *vincō.*
victor, -ōris, m. [vincō], *victorious [victor,
  victōrēs].*
victus, see *vincō.*
vīcus, -ī, m., *town, village [vīcum].*
videō, -ēre, vīdī, vīsum, *to see [vīdissent].*
vīgintī, indecl. num., adj., *twenty.*
vincō, -ere, vīcī, victum, *to conquer, defeat [vīcit, victī, victō, victum, victus,
  vincerent, vincitur, vincuntur].*
vir, virī, m., *man [vir, virī, virō].*
virtūs, -ūtis, f. [vir], *manliness, valor,
  courage [virtūte].*
vīs, vis, f., *force, power; vīrēs, vīrium,
  military forces [vīrēs].*
vīvus, -a, -um, adj. [vīvō], *living, alive
  [vīvus].*
vix, adv., *scarcely, with difficulty.*
vulnerō, -āre, -āvī, -ātum [vulnus], *to
  wound, hurt, injure [vulnerātus].*

209   Fabius recaptures Tarentum in southern Italy; Scipio captures
       Carthago Nova in Spain.

208   Scipio defeats Hasdrubal in Baecula in Spain; Marcellus killed in
       battle by Hannibal.

207   Hasdrubal killed at battle of Metaurus—reinforcements prevented
       from reaching Hannibal.

206   Cities of Bruttium surrender to Rome.

205   Philip V negotiates peace with Rome.

204   Scipio lands in Africa.

203   Scipio defeats Hanno; Scipio defeats Syphax, recognizes Mas-
       inissa as king of Numidia; Carthaginians seek peace but recall
       Hannibal from Italy and renew the war.

202   Battle of Zama—Hannibal defeated by Scipio.

201   Peace terms concluded at Rome; Scipio celebrates triumph and is
       conferred name Africanus.

Appendix A:
Timeline of the Second Punic War

The following is a chronology of all events mentioned in this text. All dates are BCE.

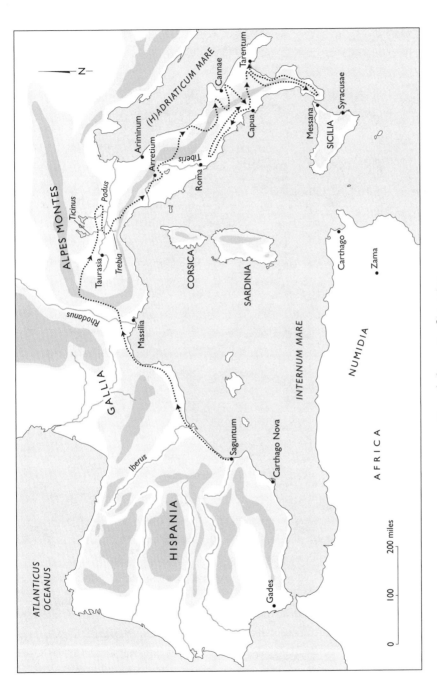

Hannibal's route of invasion

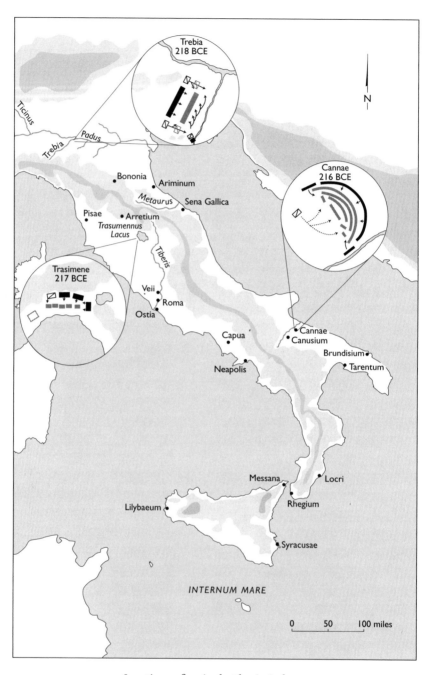

Locations of major battles in Italy

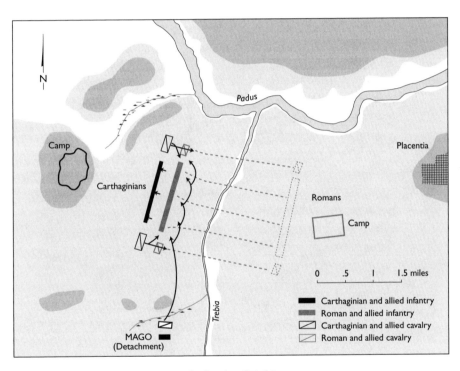

The battle of Trebia

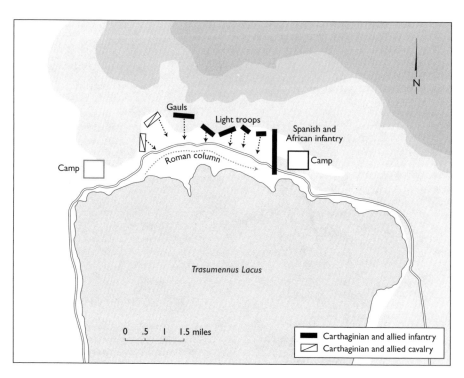

The battle of Lake Trasimene

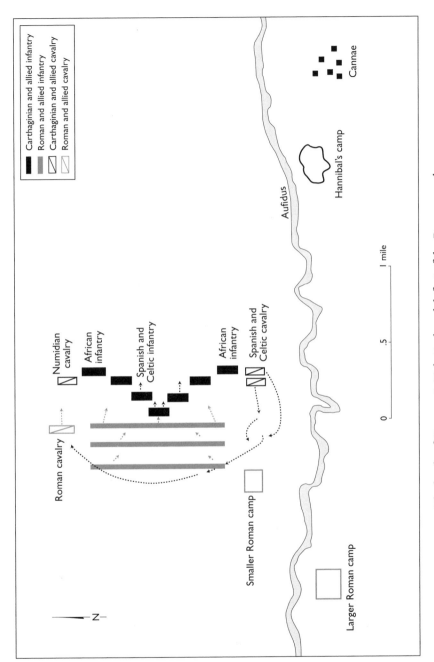

The battle of Cannae: Initial attack and defeat of the Roman cavalry

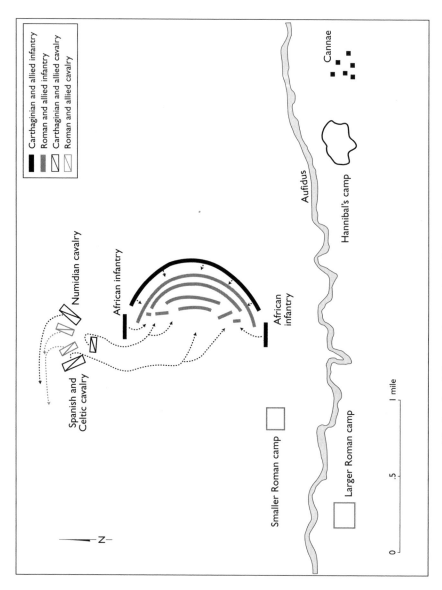

The battle of Cannae: Destruction of the Roman army

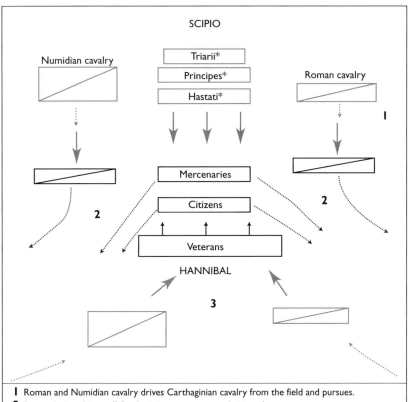

SCIPIO

Numidian cavalry

Triarii*

Principes*

Hastati*

Roman cavalry

1

Mercenaries

2

Citizens

2

Veterans

HANNIBAL

3

1 Roman and Numidian cavalry drives Carthaginian cavalry from the field and pursues.
2 Roman legion drives off Carthaginian mercenary and citizen forces.
3 After regrouping, the Roman Legion strikes Hannibal's veterans as Roman cavalry attacks from the rear.
* The Hastati, Principes, and Triarii were the three lines of infantry in the standard Roman battle formation.

The battle of Zama

APPENDIX C: ROMAN MAGISTRACIES

The following is a list of all Roman magistracies mentioned in this text. For more information, see the individual entries in the *Oxford Classical Dictionary*, 3rd Edition (New York: Oxford University Press, 1996).

Consul – The supreme republican magistrate. There were two consuls elected annually. Candidates were proposed by the Senate and elected by the people in the *comitia centuriata*. The consuls were the highest civil authority and also the supreme commanders of the army. They gave their names to the years in which they served (e.g., *M. Minuciō Rūfō P. Cornēliō cōnsulibus,* in the consulships of Marcus Minucius Rufus and Publius Cornelius Scipio Asina). By the time of the Second Punic War, one of the consulships was reserved for a plebeian candidate, while the other was filled by a patrician.

Dictator – Extraordinary republican magistrate. A dictator was nominated by one of the consuls when the Senate proclaimed a national emergency. He held undivided military authority—not subject to veto or appeal—for six months.

Praetor – A high republican magistrate, second to the consuls. At the time of the Second Punic War there were four praetors who served as judges, acted for the consuls in their absence, and governed the provinces Rome had acquired in the First Punic War.

Proconsul – A former consul who, after the expiration of his year in office, received the government of a province with *imperium pro magistratu* (administrative power in the place of a magistrate). Such provinces were called *consulares*.

Tribune of the Plebs – A representative of the plebeian order. By the time of the Second Punic War, there were ten *Tribuni Plebis,* elected by the plebeian assembly (*comitia plebis tributa*). The tribunes exercised veto power over laws, elections, and acts of magistrates, elicited resolutions (*plebiscita*), and summoned the plebs to assembly. Their persons were inviolate.

BIBLIOGRAPHY

Annotated Editions

Caldecott, W., ed. *Eutropius, Books 1, 2, with Notes and Vocabulary.* London: Longmans, Green, 1893.

Clark, Victor S., ed. *Eutropii Historia Romana: Selections from the History of the Republican Period.* Boston: Leach, Shewell, and Sanborn, 1897.

Clarke, John, ed. *Eutropii Historiæ Romanæ Breviarium with Notes, Critical, Geographical, and Explanatory, in English.* Dublin: J. Exshaw, 1815.

Greenough, J. B., ed. *Extracts from Eutropius.* Boston: Ginn, 1893.

Hamilton, James, ed. *Abridgment of the Roman History: With an Analytical and Interlineal Translation.* C. F. Hodgson and Sons, 1849.

Hazzard, J. C., ed. *Eutropius.* New York: American Book Co., 1898.

Jones, W. H. S., ed. *Eutropii Breviarium.* Blackie's Latin Texts. London: Blackie, 1905.

Laming, W. Cecil, ed. *Eutropius, Books I and II.* London, Glasgow: Blackie and Son, 1904.

Welch, W., and C. G. Duffield, eds. *Eutropius Adapted for the Use of Beginners with Notes, Exercises, and Vocabularies.* London: Macmillan, 1883.

White, John T., ed. *I–IV Books of Eutropius.* White's Grammar School Texts. London: Longmans, Green, 1887.

Critical Editions

Droysen, Hans, ed. *Eutropi Breviarium ab Urbe Condita cum Versionibus Graecis et Pauli Landolfique Additamentis.* Monumenta Germaniae Historica: Auctorum Antiquissimorum. Berlin: Weidman, 1879.

Rühl, Franz, ed. *Eutropi Breviarium ab Urbe Condita.* Bibliotheca Scriptorum Graecorum et Romanorum Teubneriana. Stuttgart: Teubner, 1887.

Santini, Carlo, ed. *Eutropii Breviarium ab Urbe Condita*. Bibliotheca Scriptorum Graecorum et Romanorum Teubneriana. Stuttgart: Teubner, 1979.

Wagener, C., ed. *Eutropi Breviarium ab Urbe Condita*. Bibliotheca Scriptorum Graecorum et Romanorum. Leipzig: G. Freytag, 1884.

English Translations

Bird, H. W., trans. *The Breviarium ab Urbe Condita of Eutropius*. Translated Texts for Historians 14. Liverpool: Liverpool University Press, 1993.

Erickson, Daniel Nathan. "Eutropius' Compendium of Roman History: Introduction, Translation, and Notes." Ph.D. diss., Syracuse University, 1990.

Watson, J. S., trans. *Eutropius's Abridgment of Roman History*. London: G. Bell, 1853.

Lexica

Segoloni, Maria Paola, and Anna R. Corsini, eds. *Eutropii Lexicon*. Perugia: Studium Generale Civitatis Perusii, 1982.

Online Versions

Corpus Scriptorum Latinorum. This site provides the complete Latin text of the *Breviarium* (from the 1887 Teubner edition) and the English translation and notes by J. S. Watson, hyperlinked to each other by chapter. www.forumromanum.org/literature/eutropius

The Latin Library. This site provides the complete Latin text of the *Breviarium* from the 1887 Teubner edition. www.thelatinlibrary.com/eutropius.html

Monumenta Germaniae Historica Digital. This database provides image files of the complete Droysen edition of the *Breviarium* (which includes the Greek version on facing pages, as well as the continuations of Paulus Diaconus and Landolfus Sagax). The image files include the preface, Greek and Latin text, critical apparatus, appendices, and indices. Main page: www.dmgh.de. Eutropius files: http://mdz1.bib-bvb.de/~db/bsb00000787/images/index.html.

TEXT CREDITS

Index of Selected
Grammatical Constructions

All numerical references are to line numbers.

of personal agent
ā Carthāginiēnsibus, 7, 46, 123
ab Hannibale, 8, 30, 56, 99, 113
ā Rōmānīs, 22, 61, 134
ā senātū, 39
ā duōbus Scīpiōnibus, 44
ā T. Manliō prōconsule, 60
ā Laevīnō, 63
ā frātre ēius Hasdrubale, 68
ā consule Marcellō, 71
ā consulibus Ap. Claudiō Nerōne et
    M. Līviō Salīnātōre, 106
ā Scīpiōne, 122
ab Āfrīs, 134
of place where without a preposition
eā parte, 13
eōdem itinere, 106
of separation
bellō, 5
ab impetū, 23
nōbilissimā urbe Syrācūsānā, 72
ab Hannibale, 125
of time when
Quingentēsimō et quadrāgēsimō
    annō ā conditā urbe, 24
Nullō tamen Pūnicō bellō, 31
Annō quartō, 48
Quō tempore, 51, 71
Decimō annō, 65
suā aetāte et posteriōre tempore, 83
Insequentī annō, 97
Tertiō annō, 101
magnō proeliō, 102
Secundō proeliō, 119
annō septimō decimō, 125
frequentibus proeliīs, 135
accusative case
  of duration of time
  annōs nātus quattuor et vīgintī, 83

of place to which without a
  preposition
Carthāginem, 6, 41
Arīminum, 16
Rōmam, 62, 73, 76, 78, 87, 110, 112,
    122, 126, 128, 151

connecting relative — *see* relative pro-
    noun as connective
cum clauses
  adversative
  cum armātī essent, 40
  causal
  cum perītissimī virī cōpiās suās ad
      bellum ēdūcerent, 146
  circumstantial
  cum . . . pugnātum esset, 27
  Cum ventum esset ad colloquium,
      136

dative case
  of reference
  Carthāginiēnsibus indictum est, 11
  sibi patefēcit, 13
  Āfrīs subigeret, 44
  with compound verbs
  Hannibalī . . . occurrit, 17
  Flāminiō consulī occurrit, 20
  Fabiōque succēdunt, 25
  Cuī virō dīvīnum quiddam inesse
      existimābātur, 117
  with special verbs
  Huic . . . dēnuntiāvērunt, 4
  ut mandārētur Hannibalī, 6

genitive case
  objective
  pācis mentiōnem, 35
  consulum . . . venientium metū, 67

Appendix B:
Maps and Battle Plans

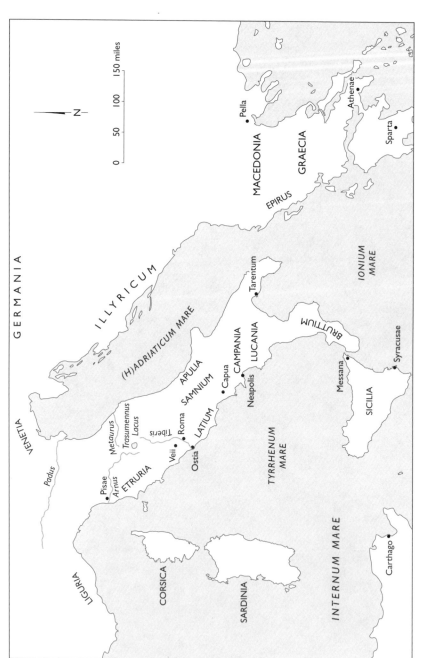

Principal areas: Italy and Mediterranean environs